1837 Rebellion Remembered

Papers Presented at the

1837 Rebellion Remembered Conference

of

The Ontario Historical Society

at

Black Creek Pioneer Village,

28 September to 3 October, 1987

The Ontario Historical Society

FROM THE PAST
1888~1988
FOR THE FUTURE

Acknowledgements:

The publication of this book was made possible by the generous
support of the government of Ontario through the Ministry of
Culture and Communications, the Honourable Lily Oddie Munro,
Minister.

Permission to use detail of C.W. Jefferys' The March of the
Rebels Upon Toronto in December, 1837, c. 1921, from the
government of Ontario Art Collection. Logo design by Frank
Whilsmith, and layout and design of publication by Cathy
Febbraro.

Typesetting by Lorraine Lowry and Barbara Truax.

Printing by Oliver Graphics, Meaford, Ontario.

The Ontario Historical Society
5151 Yonge Street
Willowdale, Ontario
M2N 5P5

(416) 226-9011

1988

ISBN # 0-919352-01-4

Contents

JOINING THE REBELLION

THE END OF THE REBELLION

Introduction

When The Ontario Historical Society organised a week-long 150th anniversary celebration of the 1837 Upper Canadian Rebellion in 1987, it quickly found itself hosting one of the most popular historical conferences ever presented in Ontario. Speakers enthusiastically agreed to be included in the programme. The number of registrants made it necessary to rent larger halls for it was feared that people would be turned away for lack of room. Unquestionably, the 1837-1838 rebellion in Upper Canada maintains a hold on the imagination of Ontario inhabitants and historians in a way that few other incidents in the history of the province have done.

Apart from the stirring nature of the events of the rebellion itself, the continuing fascination of the rebellion for Ontarians lies in the strong division of opinion over whether or not it was justified. Put simply, people continue to care about the issues that prompted the rebellion. There continues to be sharp disagreement over whether or not the rebellion was beneficial, and over whether it advanced or retarded the coming of responsible government in Upper Canada, as reflected by historians using different terms such as "rebels" or "patriots" to describe the followers of Mackenzie.

A number of recent books, particularly those by Colin Read and Ronald Stagg provide meticulous appraisals of the events leading up to the rebellion, the rebellion itself and the consequences for Canadian society. This collection of papers, based on some of the presentations given at the 1837 Rebellion Remembered celebration, is produced in response to the great demand expressed for transcripts during the conference and in the following months. The opening section features papers providing a sense of the texture of daily life for Upper Canadians during the late 1830s. The essays in the second section cover the main events of Mackenzie's rebellion, events in western Upper Canada, and links with Lower Canadian rebels and government authorities. The third section offers the recollections of a descendent of the Toronto aristocracy at the time of the rebellion, three Orange poems reflect the counterrevolutionary response of Irish Upper Canadians to the rebellion, and a list of the troops called out to combat the insurgents. The fourth section provides the stories of four individuals caught up in the rebellion. The fifth section summarises the incidents and border raids that followed in the wake of the rebellion, and concludes with a paper suggesting sources for genealogical information on rebel ancestors.

Thanks to generous support from the Ontario Ministry of Culture and Communications, the Honourable Lily Oddie Munro, Minister, publishing the conference papers in the form of this booklet has been made possible. We are grateful to the ministry for its financial support, as well as to those conference speakers who agreed to submit their papers for publication. As a result the 1837 Rebellion continues to live in our memories.

Dorothy Duncan
Glenn J Lockwood

Life In The Rebellion Era

Daily Life in the Home District in 1837

Joyce C. Lewis

In order to provide a manageable discussion of such a broad topic and because the bulk of the population was rural, this paper will concentrate on the life of a well-settled, or second generation family living within reach of Toronto. It will be a family of some education, but socially a degree below the life of the Traills, O'Briens or McGraths.

Their first log house would have been improved by some additions by 1837, or given up for a new frame or stucco house nearby. The forest would have been cleared for fenced fields, and there would be other settlers about, as well as perhaps a mill, blacksmith shop, small general store and a church or chapel. This family would have come from the United Kingdom, possibly via the United States. Of course, there were well-established groups with other backgrounds here who shared the same experiences, and they must not be forgotten for a complete picture.

One of the traps of looking back is a tendency to take a sentimental view of the past. Nostalgia makes people forget that the average life expectancy around 1837 was 35 years, and that the contents of chamber pots under beds commonly froze on winter nights.

It also is necessary to consider the legend of the self-sufficient settlers who, with one cow, one sheep, one pig, one garden etc. grew all their own food, spun and wove all the cloth they needed for blankets and clothes, made their own candles, ground their own flour and forged their own tools. Certainly the first settlers in any area lived in great isolation for a period, and relied on their own efforts, but as settlement increased and they began to have goods or cash to exchange for services, they began to use them. It is a great deal easier to buy hard soap than to make it, for instance. Working hours were from dawn to dusk in Summer (5 to 9 as we say) and from dawn to six in Winter, and the tasks needing to be done took more hours than were available.

The centre of commerce was Toronto, which many of the Home District settlers would visit once a year at least to take produce to market, transact business or shop. John Moyle, who was there in August 1837, described what he saw in a ramble about the town, in an unpublished diary now in the hands of his descendants. He found that as the seat of government, the town had a style and air which it otherwise would not possess. The streets were macadamized, laid out at right angles, and were wide and airy. There were some wooden sidewalks, but otherwise walking was difficult because of uneven, stony paths.

The shops were very handsome, many of them exceeding the architectural splendour of those in Moyle's native Southampton in England. He also liked the display of goods which was plentiful and tasteful, with the exception of the linen shops. The market was larger than that of a comparable English town, with as good meat (beef excepted) and a plentiful display of vegetables and fruit. Moyle was told that as the season progressed, apples, pears, and nectarines would be shipped to it from Niagara, 35 miles across the lake.

Two other aspects of the town impressed Moyle. One was the continual noise of ringing bells. They rang in the streets to announce an auction and they rang in his hotel to announce meal-times. From the harbour steamships about to leave would ring their bells for an hour beforehand, as well as snorting and blowing off steam while their officers serenaded the town with airs on a bugle like "Home Sweet Home" and "Yankee Doodle".

At night-time the harbour was particularly impressive. Those same steamships gave off sparks through their chimneys, while fishing smacks with lights blazing from tar barrels hung out of the boat to attract the finny tribe, dotted the water and made a beautiful sight. That was a Saturday. By next Wednesday, Moyle was less enchanted. His parents were ill because his hotel was taking its drinking water directly from the bay "just opposite where all the drains & gutters run in", and where someone had seen a dead horse thrown in. He had been over-charged by a watch-maker, the hotel keeper's daughter was wearing silk stockings when she ought to have been mending the carpet, and altogether Toronto was "a dirty little hole".

Away from the bright lights, the established settlers were concentrating on keeping fed, warm, and to some extent clean. Generally their diet was monotonous -- heavy, frugal, greasy and sustaining. Pork salted, smoked, or occasionally fresh, was the principal meat, as pigs were easy to keep and could be left to forage for roots and vegetables, nuts or even small animals. Food was completely seasonal. With supermarkets now selling asparagus in January, we forget the excitement and pleasure of new Spring greens -- lamb's quarters or cow parsley; the first strawberries of Summer and the appearance each Fall in the stores of dates, raisins and candied peel for Christmas puddings.

Cooking was done over an open hearth at first and then on an iron cook stove if the family could afford one and wanted it. This would heat the house as well, so a summer kitchen or outdoor fire was a great boon in the hot months. Frying or boiling were the most usual methods of cooking, and there were many stews because meat was tough, and they could be left to cook by themselves. Baking might be done in a bake-kettle or a reflector oven at first, or there might be an oven built beside the hearth. Later cookstoves often included ovens, but in all cases it took a lot of experience to regulate the heat, using only a bare hand as a guide to temperature.

Cookbooks were rare and those in print gave recipes for people who knew how to cook, rather than telling a beginner how to boil an egg. Ingredients were quite different from those of today and measurements inexact. Flour was often damp and lumpy or gritty. Yeast was erratic and bread might be sour. Sugar tasted of molasses and was expensive, so maple syrup was often substituted. Butter and milk would go "off" when the cows got into the wild leeks or buttercups. Eggs were small, gamey, and disappeared almost entirely during the Winter unless preserved in a solution of slaked lime and salt. Chickens were wiry, beef was tough and mutton took on an unpleasant flavour unless slaughtered carefully. Cakes, puddings and pies would be heavy because of the flour, and because there was no baking soda or powder. Pearlash might be used but gave uncertain results.

Preserves, pickles and jams gave variety to Winter diets and there were always dishes of them set out. Local foods, gathered from the wild or bought from the Indians, such as wild plums, cranberries or other berries, wild rice, butternuts, sweet chestnuts and sweet corn, would be included. (One Canadian invention was the butter tart, which we still eat today.)

Food was gathered or harvested in season and prepared for Winter use by drying, pickling, or preserving. Root vegetables and apples might be stored in a cool place, but required careful watching for signs of rot.

Meals would be eaten by the fire in the first house, but the second might have a diningroom used during warmer weather. All kinds of crockery and grades of ironstone or china were available. Common patterns were white Queen's ware with a coloured band, or blue and white dishes of various patterns including our old friend the willow. Spoons and knives were the basic utensils, with forks a second addition. Silver was expensive, but there might be silver teaspoons, or some of Britannia metal which was shinier than the pewter it replaced.

11

Keeping warm, or rather being warm from time to time, was not a great problem because the woods were still all around needing to be burned. Cutting wood was done during one Winter for the next, and by Spring each well-ordered house had a pile of about 15 to 20 cords stacked near at hand for the next season. A cord is 4 feet by 4 feet by 8 feet, you will remember. Early heating was from a fireplace, or perhaps two, not more -- because houses were taxed extra for more than two. Any one or thing at a distance literally froze. Mrs. Jameson describes her ink freezing in the inkwell as she wrote in her new Toronto house in 1837. Franklin stoves or box heating stoves were heavily advertised in the 1830s and were often in the front hall or parlour to heat the house. A pipe from it would go through the ceiling or wall into other rooms to warm them, but this was dangerous if they were inadequately insulated. Chimney and house fires were common, and in a built-up wooden town could spread quickly.

Winter clothing for women generally meant heavier material and extra layers of clothing usually worn -- extra flannel petticoats, for instance, and heavy shawls. Women didn't wear coats at this period. Knitted woollen socks, mitts, scarves, sweaters and toques would be worn but there was a great debate about the advisability of wearing wool next to the skin. Fur was for the wealthy, except perhaps for buffalo or bearskins for sleigh robes. When she went out, Mrs. Traill adopted the country custom of wearing socks, moccasins, more socks and a second pair of moccasins. Men would wear heavy socks and stout boots, well-oiled with home-made neat's foot oil.

Less attention was paid to keeping oneself clean than we are used to now. Often only the bits that showed were washed with any regularity. Complete bathing was difficult as bathrooms were only for the wealthy and eccentric, and hot water had to be heated on the fire for the purpose. Hair might be brushed but not washed, although it would be examined carefully for lice. Pomatum, or bear grease might be used to keep it in order. Toothbrushes and dentifrices to be used with a flannel were advertised, but teeth might be brushed only once a week. It is no surprise that the majority of people had lost most of their teeth by age 35.

Working water closets and earth closets were sometimes found in townhouses, but the privy out by the shed was the most usual convenience. Depending on the householder, it would be pleasant or foul. It might be emptied twice a year, or just picked up and moved to a new position when the old one could no longer be used.

Housekeeping practices reflected the energy and standards of the wife, and varied widely. Washing might be done once a week, on Mondays, or perhaps once every five weeks in Winter.

It was a heavy task, as the following "receet" shows, and the family would certainly have cold meals that day.

It reads:

"Bild fire in backyard to heet kettle of rain water
Set tubs so smoke won't blow in yer eyes, if wind is
   peart.
Shave one hole cake lie soap in biling water.
Sort things, make 3 piles, 1 pile white, 1 pile cullord,
   1 pile work-britches and rags.
Stur flour in cold water to smooth, then thin down with
   biling water. (This was to be used for starch.)
Rub dirty spots on board, rub hard, then bile.
Rub cullord, but don't bile, just rench and startch.
Take white things out of kettle, with broom handle, then
   rench, blew and startch.
Hang old rags on fence, spread tee towels on grass, pour
   rench water in flower beds. Scrub porch with hot
   soapy water, turn tubs upside down.
Go put on cleen dress, smooth hair with side combs, brew
   cup of tea, set and rock a spell and count your
   blessings." (G.M. Suggitt)

Those with a set routine would iron on Tuesday following this, bake on Wednesday, clean on Thursday and mend on Friday. All water would be drawn or pumped from the well and might have to be carried out as well as in. Soot, ashes and grease from the open fires would be everywhere.

Everyday household tasks for a woman would include cleaning and filling all lamps or candlesticks, emptying the chamber pots and scalding them, cleaning and sharpening knives (which weren't stainless then), preparing meals, washing dishes, caring for hens and geese, weeding the vegetable garden and looking after any sort of flower garden she wished, carrying wood in for fires and ashes out - unless her husband would do this, caring for children and teaching them their ABCs if she was inclined, nursing any illness and battling a never-ending parade of vermin: bedbugs, fleas, lice, crickets, moths, mice, rats, ants, caterpillars, flies, and mosquitoes. Mosquito netting was just beginning to be used about 1840, and the most common remedy for their attacks was a smudge of damp wood outside the door.

Specialized tasks might be candle making if it was necessary. Forty dozen might be made in the Fall and stored in mouse-proof boxes, or this might be done more often in smaller batches. There would be preparation of food for Winter, spinning, dying wool and knitting, soap-making, if this was still done at home, and sewing. All clothes, and anything else put together like curtains, coverlets and sheets were made by hand from material bought at the general store, or sometimes woven at home. Patterns did not exist, and old clothes had to be taken apart as a guide for cutting out new ones. One can appreciate why children were taught early to assist in these tasks and why an itinerant candlemaker, shoemaker, or other such tradesman would be welcomed by those who could afford his service.

The country woman's husband had equally full days of often back-breaking labour. There were few agricultural machines to assist him, and hired men were expensive at about $40.00 per month, so until he had sons to join him, he would depend on an ox team at first for all the heavy work. Oxen are slow, compared to horses, but they are very strong and less likely to break a leg on rough land. They can forage for food, whereas horses need to be fed grain, and in the end they can become beef stew.

Sometimes assisted by bees, whose work he would be obliged to return, the settler had to clear and stump any new fields he wanted, plough, seed by hand, cultivate as far as possible, cut or mow, carry to the barn, thresh or flail, take his crops to the market or mill, keep his fences up, care for his animals, make potash and/or maple syrup, do any building of house additions or farm sheds and barns to protect his crops and animals from predators. Bears were fond of wheat as well as pigs, and raccoons, wolves, foxes, crows, hawks, weasels, rabbits, squirrels, ground hogs, and migratory geese, all had designs on his produce.

Men not farming would work as long hours, six days a week, and might be required to work throughout the year with only Christmas and one or two other days off. Twelve-hour days with a 30 minute break at noon were common, although social reformers in England were trying to reduce them to 10 at this period.

Children were expected to take on their share of work at an early age. "A child of 6 can be useful" said Mrs. Child in The American Frugal Housewife of 1838, "and can care for its own clothes, knit garters, suspenders and stockings, make patchwork, braid straw, make mats for table and floor, weed the garden or pick cranberries to be carried to market." Older children could care for younger ones, bring in cows, split wood, goose-pick feathers from live geese several times a year and help with lighter field work.

Schooling might be started at home by the mother and continued at a nearby dame school. If the child was to have more education, he might go to a common school or even a grammar school, where his parents would pay a fee for each subject studied.

Some boys might be apprenticed to a tradesman or a professional man if their parents could afford it, or sent to find a job at a mill or nearby village. Girls might go as "help" to a family in the district. Servants were comparatively rare, and such a girl would probably not stay long, perhaps leaving to marry and take on her own household.

Despite this activity, children still found time to play marbles, skip rope, play hide and seek, or make up their own games with a few toys. Books for children were printed quite cheaply, and might be bought for a special occasion.

As family life centered on the home, so the major events of births, marriages, deaths, and funerals most often took place there. Births might be assisted by one of the midwives who were still allowed to practise in 1837. Pregnancy was not considered a medical condition and doctors were only called in if the birth was complicated. Mortality rates were high for mothers and children, because no one knew the causes of infection and there were no antiseptic procedures. Somewhere around half of all children born died within the first year. Epidemics played a part in this, as did ignorance and poor nutrition.

Marriages could be solemnized by a clergyman in church or at home, and I am not sure whether this was a matter of convenience or of cost. The bride in 1837 was more likely to wear a new "good" dress, which would be her best one over the next number of years, rather than a white one. There might be a wedding breakfast at noon or simply tea and cakes. A wedding trip might follow but more often the bride just left her home to go to her new one.

One of the first undertakers in Ontario began to practise in Niagara Falls in 1826, but the majority of deaths continued for a long time to be looked after at home. A respected older woman from the community would wash and lay out the corpse in a home-made coffin. Friends would gather with food and extra chairs, and after a service, the coffin would be carried to the nearest burial ground, or interred in a special plot on the farm if this wasn't possible. Mourning of some sort would be observed by the survivors, but the extravagant mourning of the 1860s required more money and leisure than was common in 1837.

Many shared activities brought the community together, and often church attendance was one of these. It was not important to everyone yet, but the increased activities of the Methodists in particular were bringing in more members every year. Camp meetings, held outdoors by Methodists and others in good weather, might go on for days, and described by Mrs. Moodie (herself a Methodist) as having almost a carnival atmosphere at the fringes of their serious endeavors.

The temperance movement -- "those damned Cold Water Drinking Societies" according to Col. Talbot -- began when spearheaded by Ryerson and The Christian Guardian in Toronto in 1829 and its meetings drew increased crowds. Drunkenness was a real problem when whiskey was 3 or 4 shillings a gallon, and the movement had a great field for action.

Less serious gatherings were bees, when hard or prolonged labour brought neighbours together to raise a barn, pare apples, husk corn or make a quilt. Invitations were issued, except to barn raisings, and there would always be ample food and perhaps a dance at the end of the evening.

Winter, when the roads became passable for sleighs, was the time for visiting, balls, dances and assemblies. Christmas was a special holiday, but still a family day, marked by going to church and having a special dinner, which always seemed to include a plum pudding, whatever else was served.   Presents were few and generally hand made.   A stocking might be hung up by a child with an American background, and except in German households, there would not be a tree.

New Year's Eve was merrier, particularly among the Scots who celebrated Hogmanay. On New Year's Day in both Kingston and Toronto, gentlemen made rounds of formal calls from one household to another while ladies "received" and dispensed cakes and tea, or something more fortifying.

Politics were taken very seriously by many people, and what available time there was could be spent attending political meetings, or reading the debates which were reprinted completely in newspapers. Libel laws were fairly elastic at the time, and grossly abusive statements were common both editorially, and in the field, as it were.

Public events which could be attended were hangings, Prize Day orations at Upper Canada College, parades of the St. Andrew's, St. George's, and St. Patrick's societies on their name days, plays by travelling actors, lectures, concerts, circuses, fairs (possibly with a horse race or two and some bets laid on for excitement), fires, public banquets, church parades by the local garrison in Toronto and militia day on June 3, the late King's Birthday.

So, while days were long and life was hard, there were brighter moments. Even the most disgruntled visitor admitted that for the right sort of settler who was prepared to work, there were great advantages, and that in an increasingly prosperous country, the honest labour of any man could raise him to prosperity, and a respectable position among his fellow men!

Habiliment of 1837

Sarah Walker

This discussion about the clothing people wore in 1837 will begin with general remarks about society, about clothing in Upper Canada and about peoples' attitude to their clothing. Then men and women's garments will be discussed in detail, followed by a brief discussion of military wear and children's wear.

The late 1830s was a period of economic transition from cottage industry to factory production of cloth in the British Isles. Both methods co-existed, but the greater efficiency of factory methods continuously won out in the competition for market. The spinning jenny and power loom were replacing the ancient process with faster and cheaper steam-powered production. This meant that textile costs were decreasing for the first time in history.

The social order was rapidly changing at this time. A new class of wealthy industrialists took over textile production and imposed their ideas of fashion on a world that had previously looked to titled aristocracy for fashion leadership. The masses of people displaced from their tenant farms and from individual livelihoods converged on the industrial cities of Europe and Britain, bringing a massive oversupply of labour. In the textile mills wages were depressed pitifully low and working conditions were wretched. Immigration to Upper Canada offered an alternative to depressed wages and unemployment in Great Britain.

The expansion of shipping and world trade with the introduction of steam-powered ships and railways brought imported products at a lower cost to anyone with cash to buy them.

Queen Victoria ascended the British throne in 1837. She brought a recognition of respectability as a desirable lifestyle to the fashionable class throughout Europe, Britain and North America. The changed outlook came to be termed Victorianism.

Popular artists, John Constable and J.M.W. Turner in England, led art into the Romantic Period, overtaking the previously popular Neo-Classical style. They interpreted nature in their work in its own terms as it was revealed to them. Romantic poets, Tennyson, Shelley, Byron and Keats, turned to nature and pure emotion for their inspiration. How could such an espousal of nature co-exist in the minds of people who believed in the imperative of efficiency, who strived to rationalize everything around them? Romanticism was a reaction to, and a flight from, excessive rationalization. It sought relief from ugliness by retreating into spiritual interpretations. Society even extended the Romantic ideal to include the concept of ideal woman as a spiritual creature, delicate, and unfit for practical matters. Fashion garbed her in robes, cast her in a role, to realise a romantic fantasy.

The textile industry very early converted to the devices of factory production. The cost of textiles was falling, but two areas of manual techniques persisted: the production of art textiles, for example, Paisley shawl making where factory methods could not intrude; and the home-spun, home-woven production that continued in the families who lived on a subsistence economy. The Jacquard loom was introduced from France in the 1830s to speed up and expand the scope of fancy brocade weaves. People living in 1837 still held the previous attitude to textiles, as expensive, precious commodities.

Not yet available were some processes to appear in the following decades: The sewing machine was unknown, and all garments had to be hand stitched. Synthetic dyes were still to come two decades later to replace reliance on the natural dyes of plant and animal origin used for centuries. Paper patterns were not commercially available. Seamstresses, dressmakers, corset makers, milliners and tailors custom-made clothes to order for those people who did not make their own. No synthetic fibres were known, only wool, linen, silk, and cotton. All lace was made by labour-intensive hand techniques, making it the costliest, most sumptuous of textiles.

Manufactured textiles from factories in England and the United States (after paying a tariff) were abundantly available in Upper Canadian towns and cities for those with cash to spend. Linsey-woolsey was the cloth of choice for durable work clothes for men, women and children, in town and on the farm. Canadian-made textiles were present in scant supply, due possibly to two reasons, shortage of capital, and restrictive colonial policy of Britain that coerced the colony to buy textiles from her.

Catherine Parr Trail, in The Canadian Settler's Guide, makes recommendations to prospective emigrants:

"...woolens, and shoes, however are cheaper at home, and therefore it is advisable to bring a good supply."[1]

"Ribbons and fancy goods are still much higher in price (in Canada) than they are in the old country;

so are stuffs and merinos. A very poor, thin Coburg cloth costs 1s or 1s 3d. Probably the time will come when woolen goods will be manufactured in the colony; but the time for that is not yet at hand. The country flannel, home-spun, home-dyed and sometimes home-woven is the sort of material worn in the house by the farmer's family when at work. Nothing can be more suitable to the climate, and the labours of a Canadian settler's wife or daughter, than gowns made of this country flannel: it is very durable, lasting often two or three seasons. When worn out as a decent working dress, it makes good sleigh quilts for travelling or can be cut up into rag carpets."[2]

Home production of textiles proceeded in Upper Canada among families who had the skills as long as they remained in the situation of lacking cash income to purchase their textile needs. Mrs. Traill had a strong opinion on the value of spinning:

"Every young woman is prized in this country according to her usefulness: and a thriving young settler will rather marry a clever, industrious girl, who has the reputation for being a good spinner and knitter, than one who has nothing but a pretty face to recommend her. This is as it should be; and I would bid the young daughters of the emigrant to bear the fact in mind, if they wish to prosper in the world."[3]

Another important aspect to the provision of adequate clothing in upper Canada was the pervasive custom of borrowing. Anne Langton, in a letter home said this about borrowing: she reported a wedding in town attended by her brother, John:

"...the gentlemen, from which it appears that very few wore their own clothes. This may surprise you, but not those who know to what extent the system of borrowing and lending is carried out here. Wardrobes are often scantily furnished, and, moreover the young men move about encumbered by carpet bags, and trust to each other for the necessary changes. It not infrequently happens that three or four of them dine here, all more or less equipped in John's clothes. On one occasion Mrs. Hamilton, being in quest of some stray articles of her son's wardrobe, took the liberty of inspecting the linens of a young friend as it issued from the hands of his washerwoman, where she found every single piece was marked with another name than his own."[4]

Anne Langdon does not appear to be exaggerating the practice, as her observation is corroborated by Mrs. Traill and Susanna Moodie, in writing about their experiences in Upper Canada at this time.

MEN'S WEAR

The masculine ideal in the late 1830s was a man of integrity, economic reliability, respectability, courteous manner, and religious attitude. A gentleman was courteous, discreet, strong, and upright. He framed his desired appearance in conservative, tailored, dark-coloured clothing. His upright character was manifest to all in his upright posture. All social classes, from the labouring to the professional were distinguishable in the quality of cloth and construction of their garments.

The earlier habiliment of knee britches, bicorne and tricorne hats, buckled shoes, beard, and lace cravat were worn only by the unfashionable person, who perhaps inherited the garments from a relative, both mindful of the high value traditionally placed on textile possessions. The new clothing style of gentlemen was set in England by the tailors who promoted elegance in precise fit and excellence in tailoring finish, rather than the earlier flamboyant, decorative, sumptuous styles of the previous century.

The man's shirt, a garment of comfort and washability, was regarded as underclothing. Its form derived from the Middle Ages with little change. In general, underwear has stayed conservative throughout the many changes in outerwear. The shirt parts, all cut as rectangular pieces, maximize the economic utilization of a loom-width of cloth without waste. In 1837 fashionable collars were stiffened with starch and wide enough to reach almost the ears. The cravat, or necktie was a long strip of coloured silk wrapped around the upstanding collar, and tied in a short knot in front.

Trousers reached the full length of the leg. The drop front opening was still in favour in 1837, although the fly front closed by buttons, was gaining on it. The hip area had generous ease at the back, in a style which we would describe as too baggy.

The full-skirted frock coat evolved from the earlier cut-away coat which was adapted for the convenience of horse back riding. At this period a gentleman more likely travelled by carriage. It was made of dark, fulled wool, lined with linen. Compared to modern coats, armholes were shaped high into the armpit, and seams were differently placed.

The waistcoat or vest could be made in velvet, brocade or fancy cloth. Its interior could hold padding to give a pigeon-breasted appearance, which was fashionable at the time.

MEN'S COSTUME IN 1837

Frock coat
of dark wool

Shirt
of white linen

Stovepipe Hat

Hair

Shirt collar

Cravat

Trousers of
light-coloured
wool serge

Vest or Waistcoat
of satin, velvet or tapestry

Professional soldiers of the British Army wore colourful coats of cochineal wool worsted cloth, trimmed with dark indigo collar and cuffs, ecru braid buttonholes and grey metal buttons. The coat had cutaway fronts, retaining the obsolete style after business wear had gone onto new styles. The bright colour might be said to aid an enemy in sighting on his target during combat. That this fact could be overlooked, tells us something about the accuracy of firearms at the time. An enlisted man's entire wardrobe had to fit into his back pack, or on his body while on bivouac.

WOMEN'S WEAR

The feminine ideal of the previous century persisted in enhanced form. The idealized woman was serene, gentle, graceful, modest, submissive, passive, obedient, fragile, spiritual, dependant and decorative. Anna Jameson, who railed against prejudice imposed on womanhood in her writing of Winter Studies and Summer Rambles, pointed to its utter absurdity in the Canadian situation.

In art, classic motifs were now stylish. The flamboyantly and excessively decorated gowns of the 1820s were replaced with plainer styles. However, the wider and longer skirts used considerably more cloth.

Ladies of fashion probably lived in Toronto and Kingston. They could, with a great amount of expense and trouble, dress in style according to the rapidly changing fashion in London England. A fashionable lady needed her handmaid to help don her clothes and to accompany her and manage her garments.

This is Anne Langton's opinion of the subject of fashion:

"...I find I look somewhat too simply dressed and unfashionable amongst them. I have no objection to improve in the latter respect as I wear out my present stock and get more knowledge of what ought to be. But if I can keep a resolution I will not improve in the former. If the follies and extravagances of the world are to be introduced upon Sturgeon Lake, we might as well, I think move on to Galt Lake. I am afraid women deteriorate in this country more than the other sex. As long as the lady is necessarily the most active member of her household she keeps her ground from her utility; but when the state of semi-civilization arrives, and the delicacies of her table, and the elegances of her person become her chief concern and pride, then she must fall, and must be contented to be looked upon as belonging merely to the decorative department of the establishment and valued accordingly."[5]

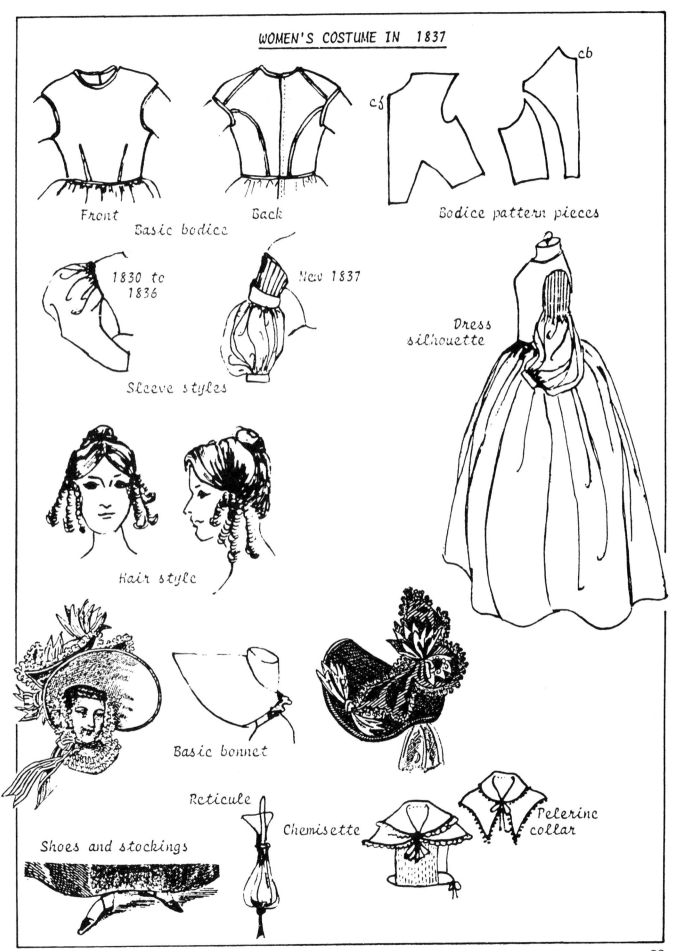

Front

Back

Basic bodice

Bodice pattern pieces

cf

cb

1830 to 1836

New 1837

Sleeve styles

Dress silhouette

Hair style

Basic bonnet

Reticule

Chemisette

Pelerine collar

Shoes and stockings

The basic bodice form of the earlier fashions persisted. It had piped seams and a concealed back opening with hooks. The year 1837 saw a change in sleeve form, as gigot sleeves, in the year before, reached their greatest magnitude. The excessive upper sleeve fullness was now reduced by pleats in the upper arm. The closely fitting upper sleeve on the dropped shoulder line might appear to be too confining, but arm motion was allowed by high-cut in the armpit area. An older dress could be updated readily by altering the sleeves, as described by Ann Langton:

> "...after which I set about reducing the cape and sleeves of a gown to modern dimensions."[6]

Later, when she describes altering the sleeves of her mother's gown, she comments:

> "My chief occupation (today) was rigging myself up a morning gown out of one of my mother's, and making a collar to it out of superfluous sleeves."[7]

Colours were soft, of vegetable dyes. Stripes and checks were usual patterns, although more expensive, imported prints were available. Brocade and taffeta were fancied for formal wear. On the basic bodice pattern, variations could be applied of passementerie, collars, yokes, pelerine and decolletage. The skirt was straight-seamed, four yards wide, and pleated onto a stay that was attached to the bodice lining. A number of petticoats and a bustle pad held out the skirt to a bell shape. In length it reached to the instep.

The undermost garment was the chemise, a knee length loose shift, with the purpose of protecting the outer garments and of giving some comfort. If it had decoration at the neckline this could show. Over the chemise went the long laced corset which gave the bosom a high rounded, silhouette. Its whaleboned stiffening gave support and ensured that the wearer maintained an erect posture and slow, graceful movements. Drawers were not considered a decent garment for women to be wearing, and if a woman persisted in wearing drawers after childhood, she would not want the fact to be ever mentioned.

Shoes consisted of satin slippers without heels. The basic bonnet hid the face from side view. Its wide brim, the shape of a coal scuttle, gave space for applying lavish decoration with flowers, fruit, bows, ruffles, feathers and lace. Other accessories included a paisley shawl, pelerine, parasol, reticule, fan for evening, locket or brooch and kid gloves. For Winter wear women wore a large woollen shawl and a pelisse.

CHILDREN'S WEAR

Attitudes to children were influenced by the writings of Rousseau. People who held to the old attitude regarding children, believed that children were basically bad, and needed harsh discipline to train them to proper fear of authority and religion. Children were workers in farm, factory and mine, who were easily exploited and readily replaced if injured. They wore the castoff garments of adults. More prosperous families looked on their children as insurance for the future. The modern view of children argued by Rousseau, was that children were basically pure, until contaminated by the corruption and vices of civilization. Reading the journals of Mrs. Traill and her sister, Mrs. Moodie, we see loving families with all members supporting each other in adversity and misfortune, and in joy. They held the new vision of children as individuals, needing guidance in the true religion and upholding high morals.

The clothing of children followed adult style trends, but in a simplified form. The chemise and ladies' morning gown, would be the closest adult models. Small babies wore long, long, gowns, like the christening dresses of today. A little boy, from the time of his first steps, to age four years wore dresses like his sisters. Girls wore shorter skirts than adults, and to cover their legs they wore pantalets or drawers. Mothers were encouraged to introduce the wearing of a corset to their daughters at a young age to ensure the proper development of posture and ladylike deportment.

Children's garments had tucks, pleats and drawstring closures to expedite letting out the garment as the child grew. Almost nothing in actual specimens of children's clothing has survived for 150 years.

MOURNING GARB

Society declared strict protocol for the bereft family members. The period of mourning required the wearing of entirely black clothes for a minimum of one year. At the end people would put away the mourning clothes, in readiness for the next time of need. If not used too many times, the clothes survived the owners, unless the fashions changed. This may explain why black garments survive in greater numbers to finally come into museum collections, than their original prevalence would justify.

NOTES

1. Traill, Catherine Parr, <u>The Canadian Settler's Guide</u> (Toronto: McClelland and Stewart, First published, 1855). p. 33.

2. Traill, p. 8.

3. Traill, p. 185.

4. Langton, H.H., Ed., <u>A Gentlewoman in Upper Canada, The Journals of Ann Langton</u> (Toronto: Irwin Publishing, 1950) pp. 113-114.

5. Langton, p. 127.

6. Langton, p. 95.

7. Langton, p. 98.

GLOSSARY

Brocade - a luxurious silk textile with woven-in patterns all over of flowers and leaves.

Bustle - a padded roll worn at the back waist to give support to a skirt.

Chemise - a woman's loose garment of cotton or linen covering the body from neck to knees; worn as main garment with petticoats by working women; worn for sleep wear; and worn by fashionable women as undergarment.

Chemisette - A collar and dickey combination worn to cover the bosom above a low necked gown.

Cochineal - a red dye made from extracting the bodies of an insect from India.

Decolletage - The lowness of a neckline.

Ecru - the colour of unbleached linen, a light beige-grey.

Fulled cloth - woollen taken from the loom and processed to shrink it into a firm, felt-like, dense cloth.

Gigot sleeve - a sleeve cut with very full upper parts gathered into puff at the armhole, and narrow at the wrist; also called leg-o-mutton sleeve.

Indigo - a deep blue vegetable dye extracted from the roots of a tropical plant. Modern synthetic indigo dyes our blue denim the same colour.

Jacquard loom - a French invention in loom technology that improved on the earlier draw loom for the weaving of patterned brocades.

Linen - a cloth woven of flax fibers. Collectively, linen refers to clothes and household textiles made of linen cloth.

Linsey-woolsey - a durable, inexpensive coarse grey cloth woven with linen warp and wool weft, used for work clothes.

Merino - a wool cloth made from the fleece of the merino sheep; a best quality wool cloth.

Parasol - a small umbrella carried by women when outdoors to shield the eyes from glare and protect from sunburn.

Passementerie - trimmings for women's gowns such as lace, braids, beads, fringe, tassels, etc.

Petticoat - any woman's gathered garment worn from the waist down to knees or lower. It could be outer or underwear.

Pelerine - a wide cape-like collar.

Pelisse - a fur-lined cloak or overcoat worn by women.

Piping - a fabric covered cord sewn as part of a seam to straighten the seam and also to create a decorative effect.

Reticule - a small handbag with drawstrings carried by women.

Stay - a narrow strip of cloth attached inside a garment to secure one part of the garment to another part.

Tuck - a pleat in a garment sewn closed along its length to take up extra cloth.

Whalebone - a stiff fibrous keratinous material taken from the mouth of baleen whales, used to stiffen bodice seams and corsets.

Worsted wool - cloth made from the longest staple wool fibres, processed to lie parallel in the yarn. Worsted is smooth and long wearing.

Elementary Education in Upper Canada: the Enoch Turner Schoolhouse

Duncan Urquhart

This paper addresses two topics. First it provides a broad but necessarily limited examination of the most important aspects of common school education in Upper Canada during the 1830s. It then goes on to the more specific story of the Enoch Turner Schoolhouse, Toronto's first free school, which opened its doors in 1848.

During the 1830s elementary education in Upper Canada took several forms. The children of the social and economic elite were either educated by tutors in the pupils' homes, or were sent to private day or boarding schools. Otherwise they went to the District grammar schools created by an Act of 1807. However, the children of the common people (farmers, labourers, tradesmen) who attended school in the 1830s went to common day-schools, which were either government-aided or non-aided common schools. The government-aided schools were financed by an annual legislative grant. The non-aided common schools were financed wholly by school fees paid by the parents of the pupils. Because so much more evidence regarding the government-aided common schools exists, they will be the focus of this study.

The government-aided common schools operating in Upper Canada during the 1830s were the creation of the first common school Act for Upper Canada, passed on April 1, 1816. By this Act it became "lawful for the inhabitants of any Town, Township, Village or Place" to erect a schoolhouse and employ a teacher.[1] At an annual meeting the freeholders or landholders of that "Town, Township, Village or Place" could elect three local people to serve as trustees for their school.[2] These three trustees were empowered to "examine the moral character and capacity of any person willing to become Teacher of such Common School, and being satisfied," to appoint the same.[3] The trustees were then required to draw up a contract of at least six months with the teacher, establish the rules and regulations to be followed in the school and prescribe the curriculum.[4]

There was also a higher authority which played a vital role in the operation of these common schools. To each district in Upper Canada the Lieutenant-Governor appointed five men to act as the district board of education. To this board of education the trustees were expected to submit every three months a report on the books being used and the rules and regulations followed in the school under their jurisdiction. Furthermore, the trustees were to submit an annual report to the district board of education in which they noted the number of pupils enrolled in the school, the different branches taught, and any other information they considered important.[5] These annual reports were necessary to determine the amount of government aid the school would receive. Between 1816 and 1820 the legislative assembly granted £6,000 for common school purposes in Upper Canada. The amount granted to each district varied.[6] In 1820 the total amount granted for common school purposes was reduced to £2,500 and the grants made to each of the ten districts then in existence were set at a uniform £250 per annum.[7] The major task of each district board was to apportion their share of the common school fund to the various schools in their district according to the number of scholars enrolled at schools. Incidentally, this legislative grant could only be used to help pay the salary of the teachers, and would only be granted to those schools which were open for at least six months and had at least twenty scholars on the subscription list. Schools that were unable to meet either of these requirements did not qualify for the grant and had to pay for their education exclusively through school fees (commonly called rate-bills at the time).

Given this background, it is now possible to turn to a closer examination of the schools and the nature of the education they provided. Pioneer schoolhouses were built by means of a series of bees, as described by Edmund B. Harrison, inspector of public common schools in Middlesex County:

> The Schoolhouses... were built with round logs, saddled or dove-tailed, at the corners, the doors and windows were sawn out after erection, roofed in with oak clap boards laid upon long poles. In some instances, the clap boards were not nailed, but held down with other poles. In some of the School Houses the logs were hewn on the inside of the building, very rarely on both sides; usually the interstices between the logs, especially when round, were "chinked" with moss, short pieces of wood split to fill the spaces, and the whole of the outside spaces plastered over with clay; but, if it were possible to obtain a little lime at great cost (for we have no limestone here) then, instead of daubing with

clay, it was "pointed" with lime. The floors were
generally laid on substantial sleepers, timber was
plentiful and not stinted, when building and
furnishing such houses. Overhead for a ceiling,
boards were placed across substantial beams in view.
There was generally an open fireplace; the back
wall was made of well beaten clay, substantial and
thick, the chimney was made of sticks covered with
clay and plastered with the same outside as well as
inside. At that time bricks could scarcely be
obtained, and the stones were boulders, and those
not easily obtained. The pupils' desks were a
sloping shelf placed around the sides of the room,
the seats were benches without any backs, and cut in
lengths to suit the dimensions of the room. Some of
these seats were made of slabs, with "two inch"
auger holes to receive the legs. The Teacher
generally had a table and chair, the chair with a
woven basswood bark bottom... there was usually a
broom made out of hickory, which did good service,
either to sweep or to scrub. Wooden pails and tin
dippers of various kinds were in use.[8]

There were no blackboards, maps, globes or other teaching
aids.[9] Furthermore, by the early 1840s some frame and stone
buildings were coming into existence, depending on local
building materials, and box stoves, placed in the centre of
the room, were replacing the open fireplace.[10]

Although there had to be at least twenty subscriptions in
order for a school to receive a government grant, the daily
attendance of these schools usually varied between fifteen and
twenty-five pupils.[11] One of the main reasons for this
variation in attendance was the common practice of trustees to
permit large or poorer families in the locality to pay the
monthly rate for one pupil, but send two or three to the
school.[12] The ages of students varied from five to eighteen
years, although there were occasionally some in their early
twenties. Furthermore, it was quite common for the younger
children, from five to twelve years, to attend during the
summer months, and for older children, whose labour was more
valuable during the summer months, to attend in the winter.

In order to try and understand the nature of education in
these government-aided common schools it must be borne in mind
that these schools were essentially schools of the people.
The nature of education the children received in these rude
one-room schoolhouses was therefore a reflection of the
pioneers' attitudes regarding education. Not surprisingly,
the typical Upper Canadian's philosophy of education was quite
limited, albeit firmly ingrained. As J. G. Althouse noted in
The Ontario Teacher: An Historical Account of Progress:

All were eager for that modicum of education which would aid them to make that mark in the world of affairs. It was apparent that a certain attainment in the three Rs was a potent weapon in the struggle for success, but success in Upper Canada at that date was interpreted in terms of physical strength, determination and natural shrewdness. The Upper Canadians were not lazy; they were ambitious. But the most coveted prizes of success lay in the realm of the practical. Parents according to one contemporary of the time, were convinced that "it is not in the nature of book-learned skill to improve the earnestness of their sons in hewing wood, or the readiness of their daughters in spinning flax."[13]

This simple desire for the three Rs rings clear again and again in school reports, advertisements and teachers' contracts, such as the statement of purpose drawn up by subscribers to a school in Norfolk County in 1824:

> We the undersigned being deeply impressed with necessity and utility of giving our children an education, by which they will be enabled to read the word of God and transact their own business - and being desirous and anxious of having a school taught for that desirable purpose - therefore we mutually agree to engage C.D. Shiemerhorn to teach said schol... Said Shiemerhorn is to teach the different branches of reading, writing, Arithmetic and English grammar..."[14]

Little more than the humble education requested by the parents was provided. Although each district board of education was permitted to spend up to one hundred pounds of their annual grant money towards the purchase of textbooks for the school within their jurisdiction, and twenty-five pounds maximum for any one school, this was rarely done, especially after the annual legislative grant for common school purposes was halved in 1820. Consequently, the parents of the students bought a few of the limited number of textbooks then available and the family shared these books and passed them down over the years. The existence of a limited number of different textbooks in the class rendered any sort of classification impossible and the result was a highly individualized system of teaching in which the pupils progressed at their own speed, with little attention being paid to grades. While the teachers may have desired classification through a more uniform series of textbooks, this was only because it would make their job of teaching easier, by permitting them to direct several pupils at a time. Certainly the pioneers of the 1830s considered the idea of uniform textbooks a faddish and unnecessarily expensive proposition.[15]

Considering the limited education the common schools were expected to provide, it is not surprising that the educational qualifications of the teachers were very low. The teachers of the 1830s and 1840s were largely people who had grudgingly taken up the occupation because they were unfit by temperment or physical condition to take up more promising work, or simply could not find employment in their own field.[16] Usually all they had was a minimum education themselves. Far from being considered members of a profession the teachers of the 1830s received as much respect as common labourers, who made as much money as teachers in this period.[17]

Indeed the occupation of teaching was anything but an enviable one in Upper Canada. The teachers generally taught six hours per day for six days per week with alternate Saturdays off. In addition to their educational duties, they had to take care of the schoolhouse, gather initial subscriptions to the schoolhouse and often collect their pay (not infrequently in kind rather than money) at the end of their contract. Finally, it was standard practice for teachers to board with the families of the pupils for one week at a time, an experience which added to the already unsettled nature of their lives.

Even the actual pedagogy must have been as torturous for the teachers as it was for the students. With either little or no prior explanation the students were given either an assignment to be followed from their textbook or some lines to be memorized for recitation before the teacher the next day.[18] In this manner the teachers were able to examine individual students at the front of the class throughout the day while other students worked away. The textbooks of the time are well known and an examination of them shows us clearly how mechanical and moral common school learning was. Murray's English Reader, the most widely used book of the time next to the Bible, contained (as noted in its preface) "pieces of prose and verse selected from the best writers, designed to assist young persons to read with propriety and effect; to improve their language and sentiments, and to inculcate some of the most important principles of piety and virtue."[19] Consequently, the children were treated to such titles as "The Misery of Pride", "On the immortality of the soul", "The pursuit of happiness often ill-directed" and "A man perishing in the snow; from whence reflections are raised on the miseries of life".[20] After this oppressive moralizing, the student could look forward to parsing, an exercise whereby "the pupil committed to memory a list of prepositions, adverbs, interjections, etc."[21] As Reverend Doctor W.A. Mackay wrote in his Pioneer Life in Zorra, the student did not really understand why certain words were a certain part of speech, rather "he knew that a certain word was a preposition, because he had committed to memory a list of prepositions, in which that word occurred; and so on with the other parts of speech."[22] Other common exercises of the time included repeating catechisms, oral spelling, and copying lines of wisdom in order to develop their writing skills (again the content was highly moral in nature).

Finally, while there are several reasons that corporal punishment was frequent and widely accepted in the common schools of Upper Canada, there can be no doubt that from the standpoint of the teacher at least, it was the only way to keep the students at these excruciatingly dull school tasks. The standard educational stimulants of the 1830s were the birch or blue-beech rod and the rawhide strap commonly known as the tawse. Numerous stories of corporal punishment and violence abound in the reminiscences of superannuated teachers and inspectors. As one inspector recalled of a school in Simcoe he visited in 1842:

> The Teacher's name was Mr. John Corkins, a tall, swarthy American. He wasn't a bad teacher, but he had a curious habit of rolling his silk handkerchief into a ball and shying it at any one whom he spied violating any of his rules, who on being struck were required to return the handkerchief and received a castigation on the hands for the misdemeanor. Another favourite method of punishment which he practised to cure boys of fighting was to make them "cut jackets". The boys who had been breaking the rule in this respect were each required to take a beech rod about four feet long, as tough and limber as a whalebone whip, and standing about three feet apart were made to flog each other well, while the Teacher stood by with a similar rod in his hand, and if he saw that either boy was inclined to favour the other by lessening the force of his strokes, he would say, "lay on harder boys," and apply his own rod to the back of the delinquent. The cure was harsh but generally effectual.[23]

Nonetheless, as the students could often be as old as the teachers themselves the latter sometimes had to fight, literally, to keep order in the school and maintain their job, let alone their position of authority. As James Kelly, a teacher of the early 1840s in St. Catharines recalled:

> The discipline in those times, as practiced by what the people called a good Teacher, was really severe. After I took the School, I heard that the big boys hurled a former Teacher through the window when he attempted to bring them under subjection to his rule. I was warned by the Trustees that I might possibly have difficulty with some of the young men -- two especially being named. One I convinced of my superior ability in an encounter which he sought, by giving him a good ducking in a snow drift, after which lesson he proved to be one of my best

friends. The other young fellow was not so easily managed. He was twenty-one years of age, and his a,b,c's as it was then called ... Having persisted in committing a glaring offence, I told him that if he did not behave, he would be punished. He paid no attention to the warning. I therefore took a large birch rod behind me, and was upon him before he could rise from his seat and gave him a complete thrashing ... I had no more trouble with him or this school.[24]

It was not only spontaneous violence with which the pioneer teachers had to contend. It appears that in Upper Canada some students savoured a curious but perhaps not altogether unjustified tradition of "licking the teacher" near the end of his contract.[25] There were of course exceptional cases of discipline which bordered on cruelty. It is recorded by one teacher that he sometimes tied the thumb of one hand of a pupil to a string hanging from the roof or ceiling, while the other hand held a book, the pupil meanwhile, having to stand on one foot until his task was finished, or his punishment thought sufficient.[26] Fortunately there was a limit to what parents and trustees would accept, and they immediately dismissed the teacher of Stamford (Niagara District) who, as a punishment had shut up a little girl in an oven.[27]

Overall, the most balanced observation regarding the teachers and their habitual recourse to corporal punishment was perhaps made by the Reverend Doctor W. A. Mackay in his Pioneer Life in Zorra Township:

> The teachers of those early days were for the most part middle-aged men, earnest and faithful, but "severe and stern". They knew little of the theory of teaching ... In the main they erred in applying themselves to the repression of the evil in the pupil, rather than to the development of the good. It is said of that great teacher, Doctor Arnold, of Rugby, that his aim in teaching was not so much to impart knowledge as to impress upon his pupils a sense of the value of knowledge, with a view to stimulating them to seek it. The pioneer Teachers were far from being Arnolds, and yet their motives and aims were undoubtedly good. They certainly did not, in their ideals, rise above their environment; and like all teachers of that generation, they had strong faith in the efficacy of corporal punishment.[28]

Education in the common schools of the 1830s was considered suitable by the common people (farmers, labourers and tradesmen) of Upper Canada. Nonetheless, there were also other individuals of greater learning who had investigated the common schools of Upper Canada during the 1830s and strongly argued that there was need for improvement in many areas of the system. Many of the changes demanded by these educational reformers were implemented in the numerous educational bills passed in the Assembly during the 1840s. These changes included a revamping of the administrative structure, the introduction of first, second and third class teachers' certificates, the introduction of an authorized list of textbooks, the encouragement of the Irish National Series as the standard uniform series of textbooks of study in the common schools, and teacher training in county Model Schools and a provincial Normal School in Toronto. Furthermore, the 1841 Act stipulated that each school section was required to raise by general assessment on all of the property in its area a sum of money which matched the legislative grant to that school section. The remaining money necessary for the operation of the school and the payment of the teacher's salary was still to be raised by the rate-bills set by the trustees for that school section.

In 1847 the first exception to the rate-bill system appeared in the fourth major educational bill of that decade. By an Act, passed specifically for "the Better Establishment and Maintenance of Common Schools in the Cities and Incorporated towns and in the several Municipal Districts of Upper Canada", each incorporated city and town was made a corporation for common school purposes and a maximum of six councilmen were to be chosen by the rest of the council to serve as the Board of Trustees for the schools within each city or town.[29] Most importantly, these trustees were empowered by the 1847 Act to determine how much money was necessary for teachers' salaries and school operations for the next year and present their estimate to the council, who in turn were expected to raise that sum by including it in the annual municipal assessment taxes on all of the property-holders of the city. The passage of this Act seems to have escaped public attention and in particular struck the council members of Toronto like a bolt from the blue.[30] On April 17, 1848, when the board of trustees for the city of Toronto presented to the city council an estimate of £2,009, seventeen shillings and seven pence for common school purposes for the next school year, the council members initially rejected the estimate on the grounds that the sum was extravagant.[31] However, it soon became clear after the trustees had trimmed their financial request considerably that city council was really opposed to the revolutionary clause contained in the Act which could require taxpayers to pay taxes for the support of schools for other peoples' children.[32] Due to the deficient wording of the Act it was possible for the city council to refuse to pay the sum requested by the board of trustees. When the city council sought further interpretation of the Act they also learned that they did not have the power to levy a rate-bill upon the parents and guardians of children attending the common schools in the City. Since the city council refused to accept the principle of compulsory taxation of all ratepayers for common schools and a rate-bill could not be imposed, the common schools were closed as of June 30, 1848 for want of funds.[33]

It is within this peculiar historical context that the significance of The Enoch Turner Schoolhouse becomes apparent. The Schoolhouse was built in King's Park, a crown land reserve which lay south of Queen Street between Parliament Street and the Don River. This area remained largely unoccupied up until the 1830s when some important industries located there. In 1832 James Worts and William Gooderham built their six-storey windmill for grinding grain on the shoreline at the foot of Trinity Street. Around this time Enoch Turner began a brewery on Palace Street near the bottom of Parliament Street. During the late 1830s and 1840s the entire area south of Queen Street was gradually populated with poor Protestant and Catholic Irish. While the Catholic Irish in the area could worship at St. Paul's Church at Power and Lot Street (Queen Street) the Protestants were unwilling to attend nearby St. James Cathedral because of its pew rents and its predominantly English congregation. To remedy this situation the Protestant Irish met with local notables such as Dr. Strachan, Alderman Dixon and Messrs. Enoch Turner, William Gooderham, James Worts, Samuel Mitchell and Joseph Shuter on July 12, 1842 (Orange Day), and demanded a church of their own. Later that evening these men met together and resolved not only to help finance the construction of a church but a schoolhouse as well.[34] Two years later their first resolution was accomplished when Little Trinity Church opened on Valentine's Day, 1844 on the southeastern junction of King Street East and Trinity Street. Unfortunately there were no funds to build a schoolhouse at the time.[35] Nonetheless, when the Board of Trustees for the city of Toronto announced in June 1848 that all common schools would be closed for the coming year, Enoch Turner felt the time was propitious for building the schoolhouse that had been promised. The Schoolhouse opened in November 1848 as a free school with room for 240 pupils and writing desks for 80.[36] Enoch Turner, in the spirit of early Victorian philanthropy, not only financed the construction of the schoolhouse himself, but also sustained the entire cost of the school for the next two years out of his own pocket.[37]

In 1850 the legislature passed a more extensive bill which was expected to clarify the duties of all educational personnel and address the problem of free schools versus schools supported by rate-bills.[38] By the Act of 1850 it was left up to the freeholders of the particular school section within a township to meet in the first week of January and, while electing their three school trustees, to decide how they wished to tax themselves for the coming school year.[39] Thus the principle of optional local taxation was introduced for all of Ontario (Canada West at this time). However, incorporated cities, towns and villages were to henceforth elect two trustees from their ward and together these trustees were to serve as a collective board of trustees for all schools under the jurisdiction of the corporation.[40] These trustees, regardless of the opinion of the freeholders or the city council, were empowered to decide by majority vote amongst themselves whether or not the schools of the corporation would be financed during the following school year by a general assessment on property holders or by rate-bills.[41]

In Toronto the decision of the elected trustees of 1851 was for general assessment and in that year the Toronto Board of Education was formed. As the Board had no schoolhouses it had to rent various buildings for the next two years. However, after a steamy civic debate in 1852 the Council decided to start building their own schoolhouses.[42] By doing so, the board of trustees committed the city to a policy of free schools for the future. From 1851 to 1859 the Enoch Turner Schoolhouse was rented by the Toronto Board of Education and was officially known as Trinity Street School. In the latter year the Board, probably uneasy with the co-educational nature of the School, built Palace Street School on the corner of Cherry and Front Street with separate classrooms (standard board policy at the time) for boys and girls and Trinity Street School was vacated. From 1859 until the restoration of the Enoch Turner Schoolhouse in 1971 as an historic site and living history museum, the Enoch Turner Schoolhouse was used by Little Trinity Church for various community and church-related purposes.

Notes

1. 56 George III. Chapter XXXVI, c. 2.

2. Ibid., c .3.

3. Ibid., c. 3.

4. Ibid., c. 6.

5. Ibid., c. 6 and 9.

6. Ibid., c. 1.

7. 47 George III. Chapter VI, c. 1.

8. J. George Hodgins, ed., Documentary History of Education in Upper Canada from the Passing of the Constitutional Act of 1791 to the close of the Reverend Doctor Ryerson's Administration of the Education Department in 1876 (Toronto: Warwick Bros. and Rutter, 1894), V, pp. 274-5.

9. Charles E. Phillips, The Development of Education in Canada (Toronto: W.J. Gage and Co. Ltd., 1957), p. 138.

10. Hodgins, IV, see Chapter X, "Reminiscences of Superannuated Common School Teachers in Upper Canada".

11. Phillips, p. 139.

12. Hodgins, IV, pp. 152-3 and V, pp. 278-9.

13. J.G. Althouse, The Ontario Teacher: An Historical Account of Progress. Doctoral Thesis, University of Toronto, 1929. Reprinted, (England: W.J. Gage Ltd., 1967), p. 5.

14. R.D. Gidney, "Elementary Education in Upper Canada: A Reassessment." Ontario History LXV, 3, (September, 1973), p. 181.

15. Phillips, p. 138.

16. Phillips, p. 139.

17. Althouse, pp. 17-19.

18. Phillips, p. 141.

19. Phillips, p. 141.

20. Phillips, p. 143.

21. Phillips, p. 145.

22. Phillips, p. 145.

23. Hodgins, IV, p. 320.

24. Hodgins, VII, p. 286.

25. Hodgins, V, p. 273.

26. Hodgins, VI. p. 135.

27. Hodgins, VII, p. 304.

28. Hodgins, VII, 1848, p. 249.

29. 10 and 11 Victoria, Chapter XIX.

30. Hodgins, VIII, 1848, p. 70.

31. Hodgins, VIII, 1848, p. 69.

32. Hodgins, VIII, 1848, p. 68.

33. Hodgins, VIII, 1848, p. 74.

34. John Pope, "The Enoch Turner School, 1848" <u>The York Pioneer</u>, (1971) p. 19.

35. Pope, p. 21.

36. Pope, p. 21.

37. Pope, p. 22.

38. Anno Decimo Tertio Et Decimo Quarto Victoriae Reginae, Chapter XLVIII.

39. <u>Ibid</u>., c. p. 6.

40. <u>Ibid</u>., c. pp. 22-23.

41. <u>Ibid</u>., c. pp. 24.

42. Hodgins, 1852, pp. 273-277.

The Ontario Historical Society apologizes for any errors or omissions in this paper, as we were unable to contact the author at the time of publication.

The Perils of the Post: Communications in Upper Canada

Joan Murray

Research into the general condition of the postal service in the early nineteenth century reveals a period of struggle and conflict, magnified by human frailty and a very harsh environment. There are amusing and tragic aspects to the story that make it an integral part of the larger story of the 1837 rebellion. This paper begins with a short description of the significance, appearance and content of the mail. Then, the transportation of the mails: means, routes, and true life adventures will be discussed, followed by a survey of the administration of postal service, with special emphasis on the 1830s. In conclusion, a review is offered of how the rebellion ruined the career of Toronto's first Postmaster, James Scott Howard.

The life of early colonists was isolated, rough and precarious, overlaid with a civil veneer of social custom and organization. Letters of the time reflected that life, in all its diversity. They are tangible records which indicate educational level and social forms as well as actual experiences and transactions. Letters were fragile links with one's relatives and one's roots. They were vehicles for property deals, bureaucratic arrangements, sales of goods, and transfers of money. Letters bridged the vast distances and were of great social, commercial and political importance. The mail service brought news of the world via newspaper and personal letter. In 1837, news of Queen Victoria's accession to the throne reached Toronto in just 43 days.

Letters were written on rag paper which was sold by the pound. It was either imported or could have been made at a mill on the Don River. The paper had to be "stout enough" to withstand transport without the protective covering of an envelope. It had to have the largest writing surface possible but be light in weight to keep postage costs low. Necessary materials were ink, writing sand, quill pens, pen knives, sealing wax and seals. Powdered ink and sand for blotting could be bought in packets. Pens, -- goose or turkey quills, the strongest wing feathers, must be kept sharpened. Mary O'Brien, in a letter to her sister, closes off with the comment, "Pen and paper alike forbid my writing more. When Edward brings back his penknife, I will try to begin again."

Envelopes had not been invented. They would have added extra expense in paper and postage. Letters were merely folded with the edges tucked in to form a little package and sealed with a daub of wax. The address was written on the reverse side. In letters going overseas, "cross-writing" was often done, to avoid additional charges.

The potential perils of actual letter writing were minor: inky fingers ... a cut finger if your penknife slips ... a blister if the hot sealing wax drips ... crossed eyes from cross-writing.

There were no postage stamps until 1851. The postmaster would refer to a list and mark the cost in the upper right corner. Price was according to number of sheets of paper and distance. For example, for a single sheet:

60 miles or less 4 1/2 pence
60 - 100 miles 7 pence
100 - 200 miles 9 pence
200 miles and over an additional 2 pence per 100 miles

For two sheets or a letter with an enclosure, the price would be doubled. Letters destined for the United States or Britain had to be paid "to the lines". The U.S. postage could be paid or not, at the option of the sender. If not, it was paid by the recipient.

In 1826, it cost the equivalent of $1.12 for a one-sheet letter to be mailed from England to York. In 1834, it cost 9 pence to send a one-sheet letter to Kingston. To check on the number of pages or whether there were enclosures, postmasters would hold the letter up to a candle flame. They were sometimes thwarted, however, by a practice of merchants writing a joint letter on one sheet of paper which was passed around by hand when it got across the ocean to its destination.

Packages of letters forwarded by local postmasters were wrapped with paper and sealed with wax. A directive in 1830 complains about "the slovenly and insufficient manner in which some Postmasters continue to put up their mails ... bad wax and flimsy Wrappers are often employed, and the packages in consequence of the friction to which they are exposed in the Portmanteaux, are broken open and the letters scattered and injured ... Strong twine should also be used to bind the Packages when they are heavy, in addition to the wax -- more particularly when they are to go a long distance, or when the Roads are bad".

The earliest known money letter was sent to "William Lyon MacKenzie M.P.P." in 1831. Double postage was charged on these letters. Entrusting money to the mails has always been risky. A directive of 1834 stated "It is with feelings of extreme mortification that the Deputy Postmaster General finds himself compelled to announce that ... several instances of losses of Money Letters from the Upper Canada mails on the Routes to Montreal and the Ottawa ... leave no doubt upon his mind, that some unprincipled person employed in a post office has abused his trust and violated his Oath by abstracting from the Mail Packets that Property which the public confidence has entrusted to the safe-keeping of the Department ... Villany may appear to triumph for a while but it is sure to end in EXPOSURE, SHAME and RETRIBUTION". This may refer to a case where Mr. Bethune, Cashier of the Branch Bank of Upper Canada in Cobourg was transferring £774 to the Bank in Kingston. An investigation of its disappearance found that it had indeed been ABSTRACTED from the mail in Haldimand by the son of the postmaster. "He was tried for the offence and convicted. The principal part of the money was given up by the thief, and the deficiency made good by his father, who at the same time resigned his office."

Mail robbery was not always an inside job, as two dramatic instances mentioned later will show.

A helpful hint to maintain the security of money letters appeared in The Patriot (February 1835). It suggested "cutting Bank Notes INTO TWO PIECES of about equal size-- forwarding one of those pieces, and retaining the other, until the receipt of the first is acknowledged; or by adopting any other means which shall have the effect of rendering the medium of remittance valueless in the event of its falling into improper hands".

There was no household delivery of mail in urban areas until 1874, and in rural areas, until 1908. All letters were picked up and mailed at the Post Office. In York (Toronto), Mr. Howard introduced private Post Office Boxes to his office in 1831. Among his boxholders in 1835 were: Dr. Strachan, S.P. Jarvis, Colonel Coffin, W.L. Mackenzie, Henry Boulton, Father O'Grady, Board of Education, Indian Department and the House of Assembly.

A list of those having mail waiting at the Post Office was published in the newspaper four times a year or posted in the smaller offices. This was useful because a trip to the nearest office might be long and difficult. There would be a large transient population. The specific whereabouts of new settlers might not be known: Addresses might read "For Patrick O'Shea, who left Cork, Ireland, for Canada" or "John Smith who is settled near York, Canada".

TRANSPORTATION OF THE MAILS

Before 1787 the portion of the British colony of Quebec which four years later became known as Upper Canada was served by an annual mail called the "Yearly Express", mainly in the interest of military garrisons. The route followed the St. Lawrence River to Kingston, thence across Lake Ontario to Niagara and then overland to Detroit and north to the junction between lakes Huron and Michigan. Any postal service west of Kingston was haphazard until William Willcocks established the first post office in York in 1800. By 1811, mail was brought from Montreal to Kingston by coach, then by horseback or sleigh to York and Hamilton. Branch lines were served by foot couriers. It should be emphasized that much of the mail in the early days was transported privately by travellers. These were referred to as "favour letters".

Eventually the system of post houses became unworkable and stage coaches were placed on principal routes. During many months when navigation was closed, the courier set out from Montreal in January of each year on foot or snowshoes with a mail bag slung over his shoulder. He considered 18 miles a good day. It would take three months to travel to Toronto, Niagara and return to Montreal. The general policy was to use roads in winter and to depend on water during the navigational season.

Frequency of mail delivery increased during the War of 1812. In an effort to guard the mail, military escort was arranged and more devious, less exposed routes were undertaken. To guarantee trustworthy service, postal employees were exempted from military service. After declaring peace in 1815, weekly trips covering the route between Montreal and Niagara were instituted, using coaches, horseback, sleigh and foot couriers.

By 1816, there were 10 post offices in Lower Canada and 9 in Upper Canada. Within the next ten years, the numbers grew to 49 in Lower Canada and 65 in Upper Canada. Mail packets (mail ships) made monthly trips from Falmouth, England to Halifax and New York. In winter, they ran between Falmouth and New York. In 1826, American packets, a line of sailing vessels made this run with more speed and efficiency, depositing mail bound for Canada with the New York Post Office. Canadian merchants, who did not want to add postage charges to the cost of their goods bound for England would send mail to the nearest U.S. Post Office by messenger, thus avoiding Canadian postal charges.

The trunk line of winter mail stage routes in the 1820s went from Montreal, west along the shore of the St. Lawrence and Lake Ontario to Niagara and Amherstburg. One could expect to allow three days from York to Niagara. There were six "cross routes": four in Lower Canada and two in Upper Canada.

In the winter of 1831, William Weller advertised: "Montreal, Kingston, and York Mail Stages five days a week. Leaves Montreal, Kingston and York every day except Saturdays and Sundays at 4 o'clock a.m., and arrives the following days." The four-horse coaches were painted yellow and carried the King's coat of arms on the side. At intervals of about 15 miles, the driver would announce his arrival with blasts of the post horn; horses would be changed, mail and passengers dropped off and collected. Eventually, the Deputy Postmaster General found fault with Weller's service, claiming he overloaded his stages with passengers and cargo, resulting in delayed mail service. Weller lost the government contract... A sad end for a man who, in 1840, drove the Governor General to Montreal from Toronto in a sleigh, in an all-time record 35 hours and 40 minutes!

Predictably, the trials of mail transportation drove many to drink. In the First Report of the Committee on Finance, Post Office Department, under "Amount of Fines levied ... upon the Mail Contractors in the Province of Upper Canada for Neglect of Duty etc.," we note the entry "Jacob Cook, on the York and Niagara route, for the Quarter ended January 1832, fined £20 5s. for exceeding the prescribed time of arrival of the Mail on several occasions at the extremities of the route, and for intoxication on the part of the Couriers".

The complete isolation along many stretches of the mail route made couriers vulnerable to theft. The Cobourg Star in April, 1831 reported "On Wednesday last, as the courier was passing the dense woods between the taverns of Messrs. Smith and Harris, on the road from Mr. Kellogg's to the River Trent", a robbery attempt was made. "Fortunately, the mail-carrier had a stick which he used to good advantage on his assailant, and he continued on his route without much more damage than a hole in the mail-bag made by some sharp instrument in the hands of the robber."

Another hazard of transporting mails is described in the Financial Report of the Post Office. In explanation for the loss of a money letter "The mail bag which conveyed this letter was lost in the St. Lawrence by the courier, in attempting to cross from Caughnawaga to Lachine; the ice gave way with the courier, and he narrowly escaped being drowned. No fault could be attributed to him, as the loss of the bag was purely accidental".

ADMINISTRATION OF THE POSTAL SERVICE

Before 1851 the postal service was a department of the British Postal Service administered by the British Postmaster General. His representative in British North America was the

Deputy Postmaster General, located in Quebec City. His responsibilities included both Upper and Lower Canada.

With the great influx of settlers, particularly Loyalists, who entered Canada after the American Revolution, there was increased pressure to make extensions and improvements to the service. Settlements were farflung, road travel was grim, people had great need to be in touch. Lieutenant-Governor Simcoe conferred with the first Deputy Postmaster General, Hugh Finlay, regarding a service for the population of 10,000. As early as 1791, he raised the question of whether sums collected from the public as postage were regarded as tax and, as such, would require consent of the colonies before they could be appropriated to the use of the Postmaster General in England. This question was not quickly resolved. It plagued the provinces, postmasters and politicians for many years.

Hugh Finlay was later dismissed as a defaulter, indebted to the tune of £1,408, although he was supported by leading merchants and the Lieutenant Governor himself. He was succeeded by George Heriot, a Scot who painted the wild colonial landscape in watercolors and recorded his travels in a book. He made genuine efforts to respond to the pressures for increased service. He instructed the postmaster at York (later Toronto) to hold the surplus revenue from the western part of the province instead of sending it to Quebec for transmission to England, and to apply it to improving arrangements in districts less favorably situated. He was directed from London to cancel this order. The British Postmaster General reminded him that the Post Office was subordinate to the Treasury. A Deputy Postmaster General could not enter into any scheme for extension or improvement of service unless he was satisfied that the resulting expense would be covered by the augmented revenue. Of course, this policy was ill-adapted to the colonies which were steadily expanding with small widely separated communities.

Heriot proposed the appointment of a Deputy Postmaster General for Upper Canada and suggested William Allan, then Postmaster of York. This would allow better supervision of the Upper Canada service and its expanding network of offices. Again, he was refused. Allan was welcome to fulfil all the requirements of the position but was not given the title. When Governor General Gordon Drummond made firm demands for improvements that Heriot was not authorized to make, Heriot took his case repeatedly to the British Post Office and begged to be relieved of his position. His resignation was finally accepted and he was commended for his service.

Daniel Sutherland, who had been Postmaster of Montreal, took up duties as Deputy Postmaster General in 1816. He overstepped the mark by proposing better accommodation, staff and supplies for the Montreal Post Office and advocating more frequent and extended service with the United States. Sutherland left office under the shadow of serious financial loss when the Montreal postmaster became a defaulter to the extent of £1,706. Thomas Stayner, son-in-law to Sutherland took on his duties. Stayner was allowed much more discretion, due to his administrative ability and to a certain insecurity regarding the legal foundation of the system on the part of the British Postmaster General.

By this time, resentment about revenue from postal service in the Canadas being returned to Britain had reached the Upper Canadian House of Assembly. Members questioned the right of Britain to fix charges without reference to the people and to maintain a monopoly preventing the people from establishing a service under their own authority. A committee chaired by Dr. W.W. Baldwin verified that profit in excess of £2,000 was being turned over to Britain. Since the Post Office Act of 1801 made no mention of colonial postal rates, the committee argued that it was illegal for the British government to impose rates on the colony for Britain's financial benefit.

William Lyon Mackenzie agitated for postal reforms. He said, "We employ a code of laws which drives the whole of the colonial correspondence into the hands of the U.S. to enrich their treasury while the British monthly packets capsize once or twice a year and charge such a price for the letters they carry that it would seem as if their owners wished the Canadas beyond the Rocky Mountains. Why expend millions on wars, and canals, and defences, and be pennywise about the postage of letters, pamphlets and newspapers? If the good folks of the colonies are wanted to be kept together, the more they know of England and English affairs, and the more England knows of them, the better for the connexion. The post office is one of the few monopolies that may be turned to great national advantage, if the rulers of the nation are not too busy to attend to such matters".

In 1825, MacKenzie presented a petition to the House of Assembly demanding full investigation. The resulting committee recommended:

1) that newspapers not be prepaid
2) that letters on public business be mailed free
3) that surplus revenue be devoted to improvements to roads and bridges
4) that the provincial legislature have responsibility for the entire management of the post office

This report was supported by a vote of 19 to 5. It was, however undermined by an accompanying letter of opposition from Sir Peregrine Maitland, Lieutenant Governor, supported by the Attorney General.

During 13 years ending 1834, £91,685 sterling had been remitted to the British Treasury, as profit from the postal services in British North America.

The question of payment for mailing newspapers was a major grievance with Mackenzie and others. Publishers were required to pay one penny per newspaper mailed. "The proceeds, after compensating the Postmasters for the collection, are appropriate under the Deputy Postmaster General's privilege to him as an emolument of office." (First report of Committee of Finance, House of Assembly of Upper Canada, Post Office Department #52 March 18, 1836). There was also some suspicion that the Deputy Postmaster General levied charges according to his political views. In the first six years of his term, Stayner earned £9,550 from this source.

Mackenzie discovered that some newspaper publishers paid very moderate amounts of postage because they did not disclose the total number of newspapers they were mailing. To avoid leaving himself open to charges of dishonesty but to help expose the system, he told Toronto Postmaster Howard that he would follow suit and publish the facts in his newspaper. Postmaster General Stayner sought to punish such effrontery by demanding full postage on all papers mailed. Mackenzie refused and tried to take his case before a jury in Toronto. His offer was declined and the case dropped.

In 1834, an Act of the Imperial Parliament was passed declaring that the surplus should be no longer sent to London but divided among the colonies in proportion to their gross revenue. Provinces should also bear responsibility for any deficit. An accountant should be stationed at Quebec and two surveyors be appointed to oversee operations, with headquarters in Quebec and Toronto. It was recommended that identical legislation be passed by each colonial legislature.

The House of Assembly of Upper Canada did not proceed with this bill. In 1837, they did pass a bill allowing members to send letters free during sittings of the legislature, an act which was promptly disallowed by the Colonial Office. In Lord Durham's 1840 report he dealt briefly with postal reform, advocating that the management of the post office throughout British North America be conducted by a central authority. Finally in 1851, the Canadian provincial government assumed control of the postal service. The occasion was marked by the issue of our first stamp, the three-penny Beaver.

TORONTO'S FIRST POSTMASTER AND THE REBELLION

In late December 1837 James Scott Howard, Toronto's first postmaster, received a letter dated December 13, at Government House. It read, "Sir, I have it in command to inform you that His Excellency the Lieut. Governor has thought proper to remove you from the Post Office at this place. Wm. Berczy has been directed to take charge of the office for the present." No reasons were given. When reasons were eventually put forward, they were vague and unconvincing, even to some in positions of power such as Lord Glenelg, Secretary of State for the Colonies. No official charges were ever laid. No restitution was made, despite extensive efforts by Mr. Howard to clear his name.

James Scott Howard was an Irish immigrant of Huguenot descent. He lived in the Maritimes for a while before settling in Toronto. In 1819, he entered the postal service, as assistant to William Allan. In 1828, he succeeded Allan as postmaster. To keep pace with the expanding population of York, Howard moved his office three times, ending with the "reputable brick building" at 28 Duke Street. Neighbouring buildings were the Bank of Upper Canada at the corner of George Street, and the mansion of Chief Justice Sir William Campbell, at the top of Frederick Street.

By 1834, he had a staff of six, and processed the largest volume of mail in Upper Canada. The gross amount of letter postage received in that year at the Toronto office was more than £4,365. His personal salary was £713. He received allowances for assistants, stationery, fuel, candles etc. By 1835, when the Deputy Postmaster General was looking for a lieutenant in Upper Canada, he offered the job to Howard saying, "I consider that you possess all the qualifications that are necessary to the office". Howard declined as he was involved in building a house off Yonge Street, south of St. Clair.

When the alarm bells rang in the City early in the morning of December 5, Howard was asleep. As he rode down to work, he saw Loyalist troops massing at the City Hall, a uniformed Bank Guard patrolling Duke Street, and two nine-pound cannons mounted in defence of the Bank. Half of his employees did not show up for work. At noon, Charles Berczy the Post Office Surveyor, arrived at the door and announced he would be staying for awhile. He proceeded to open mail he suspected as being communications by the rebels.

At Howard's home, all was not well. Mackenzie and his men had broken down the fence, entered the living room and demanded dinner for fifty. Mrs. Howard is reported as being astonished and saying she could do nothing of the kind. He told her that it was time her husband was relieved from his position. There happened to be a great pot of mutton on the fire which they emptied and refilled with beef from a barrel in the cellar. After helping themselves to freshly baked bread, they occupied themselves with mending their arms in the tool house.

According to the recollection of Howard's son, they later returned demanding more food from his mother. Mackenzie "shook his horsewhip, pulled her from her chair to the window, bidding her to be thankful that her own house was not in the same state" as Dr. Horn's across the street, which he had just set ablaze. Samuel Lount advised her not to mind Mackenzie, to give them food and they would not harm her. The rebels spent the night on the Howard lawn where they had kept barrels of whisky and carried on sporadic firing of muskets throughout the night.

Howard and Berczy remained at the Post Office, smuggling their valuables into the Bank of Upper Canada basement each evening at nightfall. Since the avowed target of Mackenzie's march was the Bank, they had reason to be vigilant. Throughout this period, there was one incident recorded which may have given Berczy cause for suspicion. On December 7, a letter was received addressed to Howard. In it was a letter from John Lesslie, Postmaster of Dundas, who had been a former business partner of Mackenzie's. He took it to Berczy, unopened. Berczy found that it was not for Howard at all, but a letter from John's younger brother Joseph, to a third brother in Toronto, with lots of rebel talk about the "just and constitutional right of the People" and Head's men shooting the "Farmers of Yonge Street". Joseph later swore that he had done this without the consent of Howard but because he felt his father's friend could expedite delivery of his important letter. Ironically, Joseph Lesslie, despite his declared rebel sympathies, eventually succeeded Charles Berczy as Postmaster of Toronto in 1853.

In Lower Canada, there was evidence of direct involvement of postmasters and couriers in rebellion. In Upper Canada, there seems to have been much less. Bond Head directed the Surveyor to fire the Postmaster of Lloydtown for overt activities. He explained to Stayner that he was aware that the usual course was to have the dismissal made by the Deputy Postmaster General, but as he desired to produce a certain moral effect by instant punishment, he was compelled to act through Stayner's agent. He requested that power be delegated to Berczy to dismiss others whom he judged to have failed in loyalty. Stayner wrote: "As regards the extraordinary power which you wish me to convey upon the Surveyor during the Winter, I do not hesitate a moment in acceding to your Excellency's request".

For the next year, Howard appealed to various officials to learn the reasons for his dismissal and to seek his reinstatement. He compiled a "Statement of Facts relative to the Dismissal of James Scott Howard" which included all his correspondence and character references. As Sir Francis Bond Head returned to Britain, he took up the matter with his successor, Sir George Arthur. "The deepest stain has been inflicted upon (my) hitherto irreproachable character; (my) family has been deprived of their wonted support, and (my) prospects in life completely blighted. (I have) used every legitimate means in my power to obtain justice."

He was able to answer all accusations with carefully documented responses. For instance, in response to the charge that he refused to bear arms, he cited the Post Office Act of 1835 which excused postmasters from military duty, he presented a letter from Colonel Fitzgibbon which stated he had been transferred to the retired battalion because of his duties, and a statement from C. Widmer, surgeon, about the weakness of his eyesight!

The Lieutenant Governor and the Executive Council concluded that, since he was not being charged with a crime, they did not recommend an investigation. "Although Mr. Howard might have been neutral as regards politics, a man in his situation at least could not be neutral, or desire to be so without blame, when the Enemy was in Arms and the Lives and property of Her Majestys Loyal Subjects supposed to be in extreme danger."

After fifteen months, Mr. Howard concluded his personal struggle. "These injuries ... are the result either of private slander to which Sir Francis Bond Head and Sir George Arthur have stooped to listen, or of some underhand scheme which has not been allowed to see the light. I cannot but suppose that the pretended charges against me are suspected to be untrue or investigation would not have been withheld...." In 1842, he was appointed Treasurer of the Home District and after reorganization of the county government in 1849, he became the first Treasurer of York County. He died in Toronto in 1866.

The Rebels at Supper, 1837

Dorothy Duncan

Neighbours and friends, I welcome you to-night to The Bird-in-Hand Inn, here in Newton Brook. My kinsman, John Finch, is away from this establishment buying provisions for the coming winter, but on his behalf, I can assure you of good victuals, ale and wine for yourselves, and clean, dry stabling for your horses and oxen.

Many of you know this inn well. You know that it was built by John Montgomery, and some of you may even remember the day that John and his father Alexander, had their fierce disagreement and decided to saw the inn in two. Alexander is still our near neighbour here to the north along Yonge Street, but John decided to leave this community and build a fine new inn far south on Yonge near Eglinton crossroads. My kinsman leases this establishment from John Montgomery and for these seven years has tried to have his larder well stored, his wine and spirit cellar well supplied with genuine articles and his stabling well regulated so that every comfort may at all times be depended upon at The Bird-in-Hand Inn.

Now please to draw your chairs up to these tables in front of the fireplace for your supper will be coming out of the kitchen forthwith. We have just harvested our fields and our kitchen garden, so there will be a kettle of Potato Soup, basins of Calcadden and carrots, and a Save All Pie, hot from the brick oven. We have crocks of pickles straight from our own larder, and loaves of bread made fresh this morning from flour ground at Hogg's Mill at the Hollow. There are firkins of freshly churned butter, and pitchers of ale on your tables. I see now that Goudrun and David Diston have just ridden in from Niagara with casks of wine from Mr. Bright in their saddlebags.

The sweet for your supper tonight is a baked apple pudding made from Golden Pippin apples from the Dalziel orchard at Kaiserville, with pouring cream still warm from to-night's milking. For those of you who have taken the pledge there will be lashings of strong tea coming out of the kitchen all in a moment as cook is boiling her kettles now.

For those of you who do not ride home tonight or take the stage to Holland Landing, we have ample straw palliasses or feather beds if you have the coin, and our establishment is at your services until the morning.

Finally, I do remind you that we keep an orderly house here, for we have no wish either to go to gaol or pay the heavy fines, some as high as £100 for accidents to intoxicated persons in this establishment. Your dogs too are welcome here in the inn as long as they are well behaved, so you must not permit them to fight in this establishment either. I beg your indulgence and good will in both these matters.

I leave you now to your supper and to your discussions. I know that after you have supped you have much to consider here this night for recent events lie heavily on all our minds. On behalf of my kinsman and myself, I wish you well in your deliberations, for our futures and those of our neighbours and friends here in Upper Canada may well rest on your wisdom and your decisions. God bless you all.

The Larger Rebellion

The Upper Canadian Rebels of 1837

Ronald J. Stagg

No aspect of the Upper Canadian Rebellion of 1837 has provoked more discussion in the last century and a half than the question of why a portion of the inhabitants of the colony chose to rebel. The answer to this question is both very simple and very complex. People rebel when they can no longer tolerate existing conditions, or when conditions deteriorate to a point where they become intolerable, or when all peaceful means of correcting intolerable conditions are exhausted. Yet to say that a segment of the population of Upper Canada rebelled solely for one of the above reasons is to ignore certain aspects of the 1837 rising and, as a result, to misrepresent the state of the colonial society in that year.

There are several layers or stages of causation which must be examined in order to account for the rebellion. Ultimately the roots can be traced to the Constitutional Act of 1791. By creating an elected body (the Legislative Assembly) and an appointed body (the Legislative Council) with essentially the same powers and making them jointly responsible for passing legislation, the Act created a climate in which conflict was almost inevitable. Elected bodies have a strong tendency to regard their views as paramount, since they represent the will of the people. To further complicate matters, the ultimate authority in the colony was vested in a lieutenant-governor. While elected members might respect the position of the governor as the representative of the Queen, this did not prevent them from resenting individual actions which opposed "the will of the people", even when the governor's action actually contradicted the wishes of only a portion of the assemblymen.

Although this friction did exist in Upper Canada, it also existed in other British colonies which had been granted representative government and where no rebellion took place. Perhaps the most notable example of such a colony was Nova Scotia, where there also existed, as in Upper Canada, a movement to secure all power for the elected representatives, but where there was no consideration given to rebellion.

Obviously it is necessary to look more deeply into the government and the society of Upper Canada to explain the rebellion.

One place to look is at the particular way in which this system of representative government operated in the colony. In Upper Canada the conflict was not simply between elected and appointed houses but also between two very different views of how the colony should develop. One of these views was represented by the Family Compact. This group, though only a tiny fraction of the population of the colony, wielded tremendous power. Members of this oligarchy dominated the Legislative Council, the Executive Council (the governor's advisors), and the senior civil service and had the ear of successive governors, who were conservative minded men in tune with much of the Compact's philosophy. Seeing human nature as essentially evil, the Compact members felt that if the poorly educated, ill informed majority in Upper Canada were given power, only chaos could result. They took as their example the United States where the people's grasp for power had resulted in revolution, and in aggression (the War of 1812). Thus they did everything they could to keep things democratic, and things American, whether religious denomination, education, or immigrants, out of Upper Canada. Although not rigidly conservative in economic matters, the Compact feared that the uncontrolled growth of the American economy would encourage men to reach beyond their grasp and destroy society. Thus in Upper Canada growth would have to be restrained and directed. Even if the Compact could not always get its way on these matters, it could block legislation proposed by the Assembly which would open up society.

To the vast majority of Upper Canadians, who saw the colony as a land of infinite opportunity, attempts to restrict were greeted with varying degrees of resentment, depending on how conservative or liberal was the individual citizen's outlook. To give one example, the Compacts's defence of a state or established church in order to bolster a conservative social order was very frustrating for a population which found that so-called established churches such as the Church of England, Church of Scotland and Roman Catholic Church, could not or would not serve the vast majority of the population, while denominations which had originated in the U.S. were more than willing to serve. Numerous other examples could be given of this clash of values.

The situation was compounded by the Compact's refusal to compromise on any issue and the petty and vindictive way in which it treated its critics. If it would give no quarter, those who were most opposed to such policies, the Reformers, were encouraged to do likewise. The Compact's reputation, blown out of all proportion by opponents of the time, for using its stand on principle to hide the fact that members were lining their own pockets also increased the animosity felt by many Upper Canadians. While the oligarchy was arguably no more corrupt than any average government, it had the reputation of being corrupt, and in government, image is what matters.

The fact that the Compact's views and actions were at odds with what a large proportion of Upper Canadians wanted for their colony and very much at odds with the desire of the Reformers, those Upper Canadians who believed that the people should control government by one means or another, did not in itself mean there would be a rebellion. If such were the case, there could have been a rebellion as easily in 1834 or 1836 as in 1837. One thing that was different about 1837 was that there was no longer a safety valve for popular discontent. During the 1820s and 1830s there had always been two ways that those citizens who were particularly displeased with the actions of the Compact could vent their frustrations. There was the Assembly which, even if it could not pass all the measures it wanted, could issue condemnations of Family Compact measures and could block the oligarchy's legislative proposals. The Seventh Report on Grievances was the most far-reaching of these condemnations. Beyond that, there was always the right of appeal to the Colonial Office and the British government. William Lyon Mackenzie had, for example, had some limited success with an appeal regarding his repeated expulsions from the Assembly.

By 1837 both of these avenues of complaint were closed. In the election of 1836 the Reformers were soundly defeated, a defeat which they ascribed to interference by the new governor Francis Bond Head and his advisors. Even though problems within the Reform Movement, such as William Lyon Mackenzie's quarrel with the Methodists also had a role in the defeat, the Reformers chose to blame only corruption and to believe that the new conservative Assembly did not truly represent the opinion of Upper Canada. In the past when the Assembly had seemed unfriendly, Reformers had appealed over the heads of the colonial government to the Colonial Office and the Cabinet in London, but in 1837 this did not seem possible. When Dr. Charles Duncombe took complaints about the election to London, his petition was sent on to the Upper Canadian Assembly, the very body about which he was complaining. This action was compounded in the Spring of 1837 when the Cabinet issued Lord John Russell's Ten Resolutions, making it possible for all essential functions of government in the adjacent colony of Lower Canada to be carried on without reference to the Assembly. The authorities in Britain seemed to be turning their backs on those who called for reform in either province and to be siding instead with the oligarchies.

The year 1837 also brought financial distress to the colony. A general tightening of credit caused by a sudden sharp, though brief, reversal in the economies of Britain and the United States meant that banks and other creditors pressed

59

local merchants and debtor farmers for payment. While this economic problem does set 1837 apart from other years, it does not seem to have been a direct cause of rebellion. The credit squeeze hit all of Upper Canada, not just areas which later rebelled. In addition, while it undoubtedly caused varying degrees of discomfort across Upper Canada, a cursory survey of the public press does not suggest that this economic downturn was regarded as a great crisis in the province. What is more likely is that the financial problems contributed to the climate of discontent felt by certain segments of the population and provided more ammunition for some men, in particular William Lyon Mackenzie, in their struggle to discredit the provincial administration.

One fact, noted above, that must also be considered in evaluating why men rebelled, is that the rebellion was limited to certain parts of Upper Canada. While evidence of discontent can be found in many areas of the colony, why did only certain areas actually rebel? It is difficult to escape the conclusion that local conditions must have influenced the decision to take up arms. With very few exceptions the rebels were drawn from semi-developed or developed townships. It was not the frontier settler who opposed the government, but rather people who had gone beyond the stage of clearing the land and building a home, residents who now expected, but did not get, improvements in roads, schools, and religious facilities and who had time to devote to political issues. In fact, many of those who rushed to defend the government came from frontier areas, where there was no expectation of immediate physical improvements and where knowledge of the political issues in the colony was very limited. For example, to the men of Simcoe County who went to the aid of the government in Toronto, the rebellion was seen simply in terms of an unprovoked attack on the monarchy.

While frustration due to unfulfilled expectations and anger at those who were seen to block political and economic change help to explain why men in the more developed areas of Upper Canada might choose to rebel, these factors do not explain why only some of these areas rebelled. Rebellion activity was confined to parts of the Home and London Districts, with some activity in contiguous areas of the Gore District and to a lesser extent the Niagara District. Although the authorities had suspicions about certain inhabitants of Belleville, Cobourg and Port Hope there was little evidence to substantiate the concerns about disloyalty, and no organized attempt to rebel. Even within the developed and semi-developed parts of the London and Home districts there was not a universal response from those who could be expected to consider rebellion, the reform-minded.

What seems to have made the difference was the presence or absence of respected leaders who encouraged their fellow reformers to take up arms. It was the Mackenzies, Duncombes,

Malcolms, Lounts, and Lloyds who turned frustration and anger into action. In most cases they did this by playing down the highly illegal nature of what they were proposing and emphasizing the moral rectitude of their actions and the dangers of not taking such actions. Most of the interpretation given to the situation in the Home District immediately prior to the uprising originated with William Lyon Mackenzie. He explained his version of what was transpiring in the colony not only to some of the rank and file reformers but also to local reform leaders like Samuel Lount who were highly respected in their areas. These men in turn passed the information on to other reformers and they in turn told others. Much of the success of this policy depended on the trust reformers put in men like Lount and Mackenzie.

What Mackenzie suggested was that many in Upper Canada were so disillusioned with the local government that they were prepared to act, especially now since the Lower Canadian uprising had closed the St. Lawrence to British troops. The Reformers around Toronto, being the closest, were in the best position to remove the unpopular governor. Such an action would be an easy one given that even members of the Family Compact supported it. As proof of this rather unbelievable statement, Mackenzie pointed out that in 1836 when the Reform members of the Executive Council resigned in protest at Francis Bond Head's refusal to take Council's advice, so did the Compact members. In addition the Chief Justice, John Beverley Robinson, had opposed a move to charge Mackenzie with sedition over his statements in the Constitution during the fall and early winter of 1837. The first action showed the Compact's disillusionment with Head, the second demonstrated that one of the Compact's leading members was protecting Mackenzie, or so Mackenzie said. While this argument seems quite weak with the benefit of hindsight, it would have seemed reasonable given that the people hearing it had faith in the source of the information and in most cases had no alternative source with which to check the facts.

Mackenzie and those who passed on his arguments urged every man to arm himself for the march to Toronto (where other Reformers and members of the Compact would join them), in order to frighten any die-hard Tories who might through blind loyalty, think of defending the governor. In this way the people marching into Toronto would avoid any violence or bloodshed. Such a plan would have seemed quite sensible to those who heard it. Most people were familiar with the armed demonstrations which were staged in Britain in support of the "Great Reform Bill" only a few years earlier. Those demonstrations were illegal but they were accepted and they resulted in an extension of the franchise. Was an armed but peaceful demonstration resulting in a more democratic government in Upper Canada that much different?

Mackenzie also looked at the consequences of not acting. He pointed out that the government had several thousand stand of arms stored in the City Hall which it was prepared to hand out to its blindly loyal supporters, the Orangemen, the Indians and the Blacks of Upper Canada, with the intention of terrorizing the inhabitants who wanted reforms. The same argument about the government using these three groups to subdue the population was used in the London District. Here it could not be argued that a peaceful demonstration was all that was needed to bring change since word had reached the area of the Toronto rising. Instead men like Dr. Charles Duncombe and the Malcolm brothers urged Reformers to arm themselves to resist attacks by Orangemen, Indians, and Blacks, and discussed going to the aid of fellow Reformers who had been unjustly locked up when the rebellion broke out.

The men who responded to these misrepresentations were not a few hundred ignorant farm lads as a later government report pictured them. An analysis of rebel and "loyalist" ranks shows both groups to be made up of well-to-do and poor, young and old. In other words, the rebels were a fairly representative cross-section of Upper Canadian society. They were not a particularly naive segment of society. They were, however, a group of men who were very unhappy with the condition of Upper Canada and were it not for their generally conservative character might have taken up arms without being prodded. The chief organizers of the rebellion, men like Mackenzie, Duncombe and the Malcolms, recognized this (Mackenzie alluded to this conservative character on more that one occasion) and attempted to play down the illegal aspect and to emphasize non-violent, bloodless reform and self defense. Their hope was that once the reform minded took up arms, they would follow through no matter what.

To a certain extent this strategy worked but there were limitations. Mackenzie's appeal worked on some Reformers but not on others. The success of his misrepresentations seemed to have more to do with the moral and ethical background of the men who heard the appeal than with any division into radical and moderate reformers. Reformers who belonged to religious denominations whose ministers urged reform but were careful to explain that reform could only be achieved through "proper channels" tended to remain neutral in the rebellion even though they wanted reform as much as their fellows who joined the uprising. Reformers who belonged to denominations whose ministers insisted there must be reform but did not say by what means and Reformers who had no religion to anchor them to the established order of things were susceptible to the idea of achieving reform by a non-violent armed demonstration. It might be illegal but to them it was not immoral.

One effect of this deceit (carried out, it should be noted, with the best of intentions) was that when the reality of the situation emerged, the rebellion fell apart. Although probably between 800 to 1,200 men came to Montgomery's Tavern, the rebel headquarters, over the three and a half days of the rebellion only 400 to 500 were left at the tavern and in the area on December 7, when the government forces attacked. The remainder seeing one of their leaders, Anthony Anderson, and one of the government supporters, Colonel Robert Moodie, killed on Monday night, seeing Mackenzie burn the home of Robert Horne and trying to burn the house of Sheriff W.B. Jarvis on Tuesday and finding the defenders of Toronto prepared to fight on Tuesday evening, had gone home. Similarly, in the London District, it was difficult to decide what to do with the 500 rebels assembled since they thought they were there essentially to defend themselves. After almost a week of marching about the countryside, Duncombe's party learned that forces loyal to the government were descending on them, and dispersed.

Mackenzie might have succeeded at Toronto, at least in the short run, had he been a better military leader and thus able to take the city quickly and with little fighting. Had that happened it is entirely possible that more of those who anxiously desired reform might have joined him in the belief that change could be achieved by a peaceful demonstration of forceful resolve. Duncombe's men might then have been persuaded to march into Hamilton or London. When Mackenzie's unsuccessful attempt to take the city led to bloodshed it is not surprising, given the nature of Upper Canadian society, that the rebellion would fail.

What was lacking was not the desire to have reform but the resolve to fight and to kill in order to get reform. It is possible to admire men like Mackenzie and Duncombe who felt so strongly that Upper Canada had to be freed that they did everything they could to bring about a rebellion. One can admire that small group of men at Montgomery's Tavern who decided that Mackenzie was right and that it was worth fighting and dying for Upper Canada. Yet one must also admire those men like Samuel Lount and David Gibson who stayed with the rebels after they discovered the deception and attempted to carry out the idea of a non-violent, bloodless change of government, and respect those men who came to Montgomery's Tavern but decided that reform, however desirable, was not worth killing their fellow citizens and creating a civil war.

Events in the Western District, 1838: The Other Rebellion

John C. Carter

The bulk of written evidence concerning the events of the rebellion period present a Toronto-centred viewpoint which pays little attention to local events in other regions of the two colonies. The intent of this paper is to examine events taking place in Essex County during 1838, commonly referred to as the "Patriot Wars", that threw the western frontier and the province at large into turmoil. They constitute an integral part of our province's history and must therefore be elevated to their proper place of significance in Ontario's recorded past.

Both rebellions in Upper and Lower Canada were hastily conceived, poorly planned and executed. Against staggering odds, efforts by Papineau and Mackenzie to wrest control from the governing class were destined for defeat.

Mackenzie's last desperate act for "freedom" on Navy Island came to an end with evacuation on January 13, 1838. Criticism of the Patriots' motives came from many quarters. A scathing attack was sent by gadfly Robert Gourlay to the commander in chief of the Patriot forces, Rensselaer Van Rensselaer:

> Never was hallucination more blinding than yours. At a moment of profound peace, putting on armour, and, led by the little editor of the blackguard newspaper, entering the lists of civil broil, and erecting your standard on Navy Island to defy the armies of Britain! David before Goliath seemed little; but God was with him. What are you, in the limbo of vanity, with no stay but the devil.[1]

The Patriot cause however was not dead. Numerous volunteers were still enlisting in the United States. Many American sympathizers from Ohio, Pennsylvania and Michigan swelled the Patriot ranks. Centres of support for the "cause of liberty" were found in Buffalo, Rochester and Lockport in the east, and Detroit, Cleveland and Port Huron in the west.

Canadian refugees and American Patriots banded together in an attempt to "liberate" Canada from British rule. Without any official sanction, local committees were established to collect provisions and arms to assist the Canadian populace, which was seen in some quarters as being an "injured and oppressed people."

Patriot volunteers were organized into armies with the intent of invading Canada to overthrow a "century of British persecution". General Donald McLeod, a Canadian refugee and veteran of the War of 1812, was appointed commander-in-chief of the western division of the Patriot Army.[2]

Supporters of American-style democracy, Canadian expatriates in search of adventure, and remnants of Mackenzie's rag-tag rebel army joined in renewed efforts to overthrow the government of Upper Canada. The Patriots counted on discontent in other portions of the province as well as continued faith in the principles of freedom and liberty to further their cause. Robert Marsh, a resident of St. Catharines and Chippewa, joined Mackenzie on Navy Island. He reflected the feelings of many of the Patriots in his remembrances about the events of this period:

> It was all excitement in Buffalo, Cleveland, Detroit and all along the Frontier, as well as Lockport, Rochester, and in fact, the whole country was awake; many and strong were the inducements for young, as well as married men, to engage in so glorious a cause.[3]

The threat to peace now came from an external source. Residents in Essex County had to face pressures initiated from without. Reform was one issue but rebellion was another. Did Patriot motives deal with Canadian liberty or were they in fact, intended to precipitate an American conquest? The fire of revolt had been rekindled in the Western District. It would soon burst into flame as the Patriot Wars.

By the end of the first week of January 1838, several hundred Patriots had gathered at various points along the Detroit River. Raids at Monroe and Detroit on government arsenals had netted more than 800 stand of arms. Michigan officials sought to discourage Patriot plans. Brigadier General Hugh Brady, commandant for the Northwestern Military Department of the United States, federalized a 52 man contingent of Detroit militia. They were to stand guard over the Dearbornsville arsenal and the Detroit magazine to prevent any further plundering. Feelings continued to run high. On January 6, the Patriots seized the schooner Anne, loaded it with stolen ordnance and sailed downriver for Gibralter, Michigan.

On reaching Gibralter this force met other Patriot troops from Cleveland under the direction of General Thomas Jefferson Sutherland.[4] Sutherland assumed command of the Patriot forces and appointed Detroit druggist Edward Theller to command the Anne.

United States federal marshalls and Michigan Governor Stephens T. Mason attempted to confront the Patriots and order their surrender, but failed. Theller, in a contemporary account, explained that January 6 was chosen to launch an assault on the Western District as there were no regular British troops occupying Sandwich, Windsor or Malden. These places were protected only by members of the provincial militia. The Patriot forces were determined to make a landing believing that if a provisional government could be established and maintained for a week, that additional recruits could be counted upon to successfully repel any attack mounted by British regulars.

The Patriot force totalling approximately 300 men, moved to Sugar Island January 8. Here preparations were made for an assault on nearby Canadian Bois Blanc Island. During the day the Anne weighed anchor and sailed past Amherstburg firing shots from her cannon into town. Edward Theller recalled that there was great excitement among the inhabitants and troops on the Canadian shore. From his vantage point on the deck of the Anne, he noted that:

> The church bells were ringing, drums beating; officers galloping to and fro along the shore, and urging crowds of people to repel the attack, which they no doubt believed our vessel was about making on the town. All seemed bustle and confusion.[5]

On the morning of January 9, the Patriot army occupied Bois Blanc Island. The invaders met with no resistance as Canadian forces had evacuated the previous day fearing that the Patriots might take advantage of the absence of the militia from Amherstburg, and attack the town undefended. John Prince, colonel of the Third Essex Regiment and a magistrate for the Western District, chronicled the evacuation in his January 8 diary entry:

> A fine day and much Snow on the Ground. We left the Island for a few hours in the morning. About 3 p.m., alarm was given that the Enemy had set sail from Sugar Island and was about landing on Enemy (2 or 300) coming over. Watched them 3 hours but they hovered about the Island and kept off. We thought

they meant to take Malden, and we therefore evacuated the Island and returned to Town.[6]

General Sutherland's version of his troops' capture of Bois Blanc Island differed immensely from the account provided by Colonel Prince. The Patriot general described the action as if it was a complete rout of defending forces:

> So precipitate were the enemy to get beyond the reach of our guns, they ran off, leaving us most of their camp equipage -- a large quantity of provisions and stores, with some munitions.[7]

The Patriot tri-coloured flag was raised and General Sutherland issued a proclamation calling upon Canadians to join Patriot forces, and to free themselves from the "tyranny of the British Crown."

On the evening of January 9, the schooner _Anne_ weighed anchor and proceeded down the Detroit River preparing to bombard Amherstburg and Fort Malden. Once opposite the town some 12 to 14 cannon shots were fired. The militia and volunteers followed the schooner along the Canadian shoreline and peppered the Patriot vessel with musket shot. Opposite Elliot's Point the schooner lost its steering, became unmanageable, and went aground. Members of the Kent and Essex militia waded into the icy waters of the Detroit River to capture the disabled schooner. The boarding party was not challenged, and the _Anne_ was captured without further incident. Edward Theller surrendered his command and described the defeat in the following manner:

> Many of our men were wounded and considerable damage done to the rigging. Captain Davis, who was holding on to the anchor, was shot in the wrist and the groin, of which he afterwards died, and away went the anchor. The enemy aimed with fatal precision at the helmsman, and he fled below, leaving the boat to her own will, and as the down-hauls had been cut away by the shot, the sails could not be managed. Unskilled as mariners, confusion reined among us; and the schooner drifting with the ice, we were a few moments aground on the main shore, our deck presenting an inclined front to the irritated and triumphant marksmen of the enemy.[8]

A total of 21 prisoners were taken along with 300 muskets, 10 kegs of powder, three cannon and other miscellaneous armaments.

The Canadians braced themselves in anticipation of another assault the next day as General Sutherland issued a declaration threatening the "horrors of War" to all who resisted the rebel efforts of "liberation". He called upon residents of the Western District to lay down their arms and to return to their homes. After this bold pronouncement, it was Sutherland however who ordered his troops to fall back to Sugar Island. The Patriot general then inexplicably returned to Detroit.

General Henry S. Handy arrived later that day to take stock of the Patriot situation. By vote of the troops, Handy took command. He remained on Sugar Island for several days waiting for additional munitions to arrive and spent time drilling his charges. No new military supplies were forthcoming and changing ice conditions in the Detroit River threatened to cut off any means of escape. Michigan Governor Mason responded to a petition for assistance from General Handy and proceeded to Sugar Island by boat. Nearly 300 Patriots were ferried back to Gibralter, where weapons were confiscated and troops dispersed. Remaining undaunted, Patriot leaders immediately began preparations for another attack upon Fort Malden. Remnants of the Patriot brigades were drilled without arms near Gibralter. Several attempts were made to acquire more munitions without success. Internal feuding between Generals Handy and Sutherland resulted in ultimate failure of this project.

The collapse of Patriot plans for another invasion of the Western District defused an extremely tense situation. The frustration of the Patriot hierarchy was echoed in General Handy's manuscript report of the previous actions:

> Thus was the third and last arrangement to carry out the campaign broken up by treachery or ignorance.[9]

By mid-January a relative calm had returned to the Detroit River region. Although initial attempts by Patriot forces to invade the Western District had proven to be disastrous, Patriot leaders remained confident of future successes. Even warnings from imprisoned colleagues could not dissuade General Sutherland from planning another incursion set for late February. Patriot W.W. Dodge, who had been seized during the schooner Anne fiasco and who was incarcerated at Amherstburg, wrote to Sutherland on January 13. Dodge suggested that Upper Canadians were not disaffected with their system of government, and to continue the "war of liberation" would be folly. He concluded his plea to the general by noting the following:

> To gain the point we aimed at is utterly impossible. To prevent further blood-shed is our duty. Nothing can be gained by further hostile operations, and as your friend and comrade engaged, as I foolishly thought in the cause of liberty - an opinion based upon false reports and misrepresentations - I again implore you to separate - to return home and to abandon a cause so utterly hopeless, and as I now perceive, so thoroughly unjust.[10]

Despite such warnings, Patriot leaders continued to prepare for a two-pronged attack planned for February 22. These actions coincided with the celebration of George Washington's birthday. One detachment under the command of Colonel H.C. Seward invaded Pelee Island. This was meant to be a diversion to allow Patriot troops headed by Generals McLeod and Ashley and Colonel Wilcox to attack and capture Fort Malden. As preparations for these assaults began, the jingoistic war of words between the two adversaries continued unabated. In the January 23 edition of the <u>Sandwich Western Herald</u>, the Canadian position was presented:

> Away ye American sympathizers with the ridiculous notion of imposing upon a <u>free</u> and <u>loyal</u> people the detestable bonds of Republicanism! We want none of your boasted self-eulogized Constitution. We want none of your laws and <u>Sovereign Mob</u> law breakers.[11]

In Detroit the town guard patrolled the city and river banks taking appropriate measures to preserve neutrality. General Hugh Brady took strenuous steps to protect the peace. An alarm system to notify the civic soldiery of impending unrest was established. The stage was set for a series of occurrences that would take place during the latter part of February 1838. These forays would again challenge Canadian sovereignty and constitute an important episode in the Patriot Wars in the Western District. Whether to remain loyal to the British Crown or to accept U.S. republicanism would become the dominant issues for residents of Essex County to contend with.

In February, tensions across the river in Detroit again signalled impending upheaval. Three false alarms were rung from the bell of the downtown Presbyterian church. A fourth alarm tolled on the evening of February 23. American authorities discovered that arms and supplies were being loaded onto the steamer <u>Erie</u> by Patriot supporters. Preparations for an assault on Upper Canadian Fighting Island now began in earnest. Once loaded, the steamer embarked downriver toward its destination. Patriot forces arrived from Toledo and Cleveland and began marshalling at Gibralter under the direction of Donald McLeod. These troops were joined by a detachment of sympathizers from Detroit led by General Sutherland.

Word of the gathering resulted in American troops being sent downriver. On February 24, a contingent commanded by Major John Garland, reached Ecorse. Here they found that the Patriot forces had already crossed the frozen Detroit River and had taken possession of Fighting Island. The Patriots' military position was particularly perilous. While they had encountered no resistance in their conquest, they were severely limited in firepower. Arms were at a premium and General McLeod sent an urgent dispatch to Colonel D.D. McKinney in Monroe, detailing his position:

The Patriot forces that were here have crossed into Canada, this day, but lack arms and ammunition. You will send all munitions of war, that you have on hand and can collect, immediately here to be forwarded across the River. You will also urge on the men from the different places without delay to join the main body.[12]

Dr. Charles Duncombe who had recently arrived in Detroit after his abortive attempt at rebellion in the London District, issued a public notice which was intended to garner support for McLeod's party on Fighting Island:

The patriots under command of General D. McLeod, hoisted the standard of liberty in Upper Canada. He delivered a short and spirited address to the men, in which, after briefly relating the evils of an irresponsible government, the oppression of the people in Upper Canada, concluded by adding that their present object was undertaken in defence of the inalienable rights of man, and to extend to their suffering Canadian brethren the engagement of equal rights and the civil and religious liberty.[13]

This appeal resulted in the procurement of forty additional muskets, of which 35 were serviceable. These weapons were immediately conveyed to General McLeod for his use.

Patriot plans were a poorly kept secret. General Hugh Brady was advised of the Patriots' actions and informed Colonel John Maitland, commandant at Fort Malden. Government officials in Toronto had been aware of the impending invasion for several days. Patriot intentions were well known, [14] and this information resulted in a quick response by Canadian defenders.

Before daylight on the morning of February 25, the Kent militia under Lieutenant Baby's command, and other militia from Sandwich assembled at Petite Cote. Here they were joined by several companies of the 24th British regiment, headed by Major H.D. Townshend. Townshend decided to make a direct attack on the invaders. Volleys of grape shot and a steady artillery barrage preceded this assault. Major Townshend related the details of the attack in an account published in the Toronto <u>Patriot</u>. In his February 25 dispatch to Colonel Maitland, Townshend noted that:

This advance was executed with regularity and order, and I only regret that the enemy did not give us the opportunity of disproving to the American nation and the rebels who have so actively disseminated the libel 'that the Militia of the Upper Province would not fight against them', as I can safely say I never witnessed more alacrity and zeal than was shown on their foul aspersers.[15]

Outnumbered and outgunned, General McLeod ordered his troops to retreat to the American side. Here many Patriots were disarmed by the Brady Guards, arrested, and transported back to Detroit. Reports of the casualties and the actual events that took place on Fighting Island varied. The engagement was satirised in a mocking broadside entitled "Yankee Song of Triumph", printed in the March 2 edition of the Toronto Patriot:

> Let our victorious banners fly,
> And give our bugles breath:
> Forward! and let the battle-cry
> Be victory or death!
>
> But what is yonder dashing cloud?
> And what in bold array?
> THE BRITONS COME! lord: what a crowd!
> GOOD GOD! LET'S RUN AWAY[16]

A different description was given by Patriot observers. A discouraged Donald McLeod reported from his sanctuary in Sandusky, Ohio, that:

> The Patriot forces under my immediate command have been defeated, but not disgraced... We sustained ourselves for four hours against 500 British Regulars and then did not leave the field, till nearly surrounded by them.[17]

The Michigan press viewed the Fighting Island episode as the Patriots' "death knell." General Hugh Brady concurred. In a February 26 dispatch to his superior General Winfield Scott, Brady suggested that the Patriots "Must soon be convinced, if they are not already, of the utter futility of such an undertaking and will disperse and return to their homes."[18] Patriot supporters were however exhorted by their leaders not to lose faith in the cause and were urged to press on with their efforts of "liberation." In a circular sent to sympathizers, Acting Adjutant General R.W. Ashley Jr. wrote:

> Let not this misfortune of the Patriot Army, dampen the feelings you entertained for the cause in the commencement of the struggle. It is only a temporary defeat. In the American Revolution the people of the Colonies suffered similar disasters, and I trust that the patriots of Canada will be cheered as they were, by the crossing of the Delaware. Emphatically, this is the winter of our discontent -- the winter of '77. The forlorn hope in Canada may yet dispel the gloom which now pervades the countenances of every lover of freedom,

and may scatter the cloud of darkness which now hangs over our heads.[19]

Patriot leaders still held firm the belief that Canada would eventually become a "free and independent nation" through their efforts. Reluctant to accept his defeat on Fighting Island, McLeod regrouped in Lower Sandusky. Intent on joining Patriot Forces commanded by Colonel Seward on Pelee Island, McLeod forwarded a dispatch to Colonel Wilcox in Detroit to collect and march men to bolster Seward's contingent. Seward was sent orders to fortify his position and to remain on Pelee Island until McLeod's forces and those from Detroit could join him.[20]

Support for the Patriot cause remained high along the southern shore of Lake Erie. An article in the February 12, 1838 edition of the <u>Cleveland Daily Advertiser</u> estimated that a force of between 700 and 1,500 men had assembled to further the Patriot cause. On February 25, 400 of these troops crossed the frozen expanse of Lake Erie and seized property on Pelee Island owned by William McCormick. During the following week additional recruits arrived, arms were distributed, and time was spent in constant drilling exercises. Shortly after occupation, word was sent to Colonel Maitland at Amherstburg. A reconnaissance party was dispatched on March 1 to advise whether or not to move troops over the ice to dislodge the rebel invaders. On receiving positive notification, Colonel Maitland, accompanied by four companies of regular troops, a detachment of cavalry, members of the Essex volunteer militia, and a small party of Indians set out on the thirty-five mile journey. After a brief respite at Colchester, the expedition proceeded across Pidgeon Bay to Pelee Island. Colonel John Prince who mustered with the loyal troops, chronicled the details of the adventure in his dairy:

> At 3 p.m. I recd. a message from the Honble Colonel Maitland to march to Point Pelee Island to fight the Invaders there. Set out at 4 p.m. & travelled all night long...reached Point Pelee Island with the Troops just after Sun-rise. Occupied the island at once. Released the Inhabitants who were prisoners to the Rebels & Invaders. The Latter fled![21]

The released captives informed Colonel Maitland that the enemy numbered approximately four hundred. Maitland faced a dilemma. If he kept his forces intact and swept across the island, the Patriots could escape. Plans were formulated to prevent such flight and a detachment headed by Captain Brown split off from the main body of troops and moved to a point on the southern end of the island. Here they took up a defensive position to intercept and to cut off the expected Patriot retreat. As anticipated the Patriot forces began to emerge from the woods and were soon engaged in a brisk fusillade with the British regulars. The scene was graphically portrayed by trooper Samuel Williams of the St. Thomas Cavalry:

> As we proceeded we saw the sleighs retreat, and the soldiers were strung out in a line across the ice, like fence posts. The enemy were approaching them at a quick march. We could not see them just at first. They approached Captain Brown's force in solid column, and then spread out in a line about the same length as that of the British infantry ... The infantry charged with fixed bayonets at that moment in the face of heavy fire from the enemy. When the infantry were within about six rods of the enemy, the latter retreated in disorder, running like wild turkeys every way.[22]

The battle was recorded in a different light by Patriot Colonel E.D. Bradley. In an express to general Sutherland on March 4, the defeat of the rebel forces was announced in the following manner:

> A bloody contest ensued, the patriots numbering only 152, the British full 500. After fifteen minutes hard fighting, the British lines began to waver and were on the point of retreating such was the havoc our rifles made in their ranks, when Col. Maitland with 600 regulars and two field pieces, was discovered pressing on our right flank, to cut off our retreat. This turned the fortune of the day. We were obliged to retreat to the American shore.[23]

Escaping Patriots were met by General Hugh Brady and a company of Ohio militia on the U.S. side. Weapons were confiscated, the group disbanded, and individuals allowed to return to their homes. British forces scoured the woods for several hours prior to reforming company and proceeding back to Amherstburg with the wounded and captured Patriot prisoners.

The objectives of liberating Pelee Island from "brigands", restoring it to William McCormick, and defeating the enemy and sending it into retreat had all been achieved. Colonel Maitland in the March 4 communique to his commander Colonel Foster, reported:

> I regret to say that the taking of this Island has not been gained without considerable loss on our part, and I have to request that you will report for his Excellency's information, that 30 soldiers from the 32nd Regiment fell in this affair, 2 of whom were killed, the others, some dangerously, some seriously wounded. I sincerely regret the loss of so many brave soldiers and feel it more, when I reflect that they did not fall before an honourable

enemy, but under the fire of a desperate gang of murderers and marauders.[24]

A final blow to the Patriot cause came with the capture of General Thomas Sutherland and his aide-de-camp, Captain Patrick Spencer. On his return from Pelee Island on March 4, Colonel John Prince observed the Patriot general travelling on the ice some seven miles below Amherstburg. After a long chase, Prince captured his quarry and conveyed the prisoners to Fort Malden. This event marked the final act of the Battle of Pelee Island.

An ironic footnote was provided when General Donald McLeod wrote to the mother of a fallen comrade on March 12, still indicating that a desire for "freedom" for Canadians was his primary goal:

> Dear Madam: I have just arrived in town, and it is with great pain that I announce to you the death of your brave and heroic son, Henry Van Rensselaer, at the Battle of Pelee Island. He died cheering on his men to victory. When Canada becomes free, I assure you, a monument shall be erected to your brave and chivalrous son.[25]

As the "battle on the ice" came to an end, there was only one final event in the Patriot Wars in Essex County. British troops had saved the Western District from foreign occupation at Pelee Island, yet few on either side were ready to concede that hostilities had come to a complete and lasting end.

With the capture of the schooner Anne and defeats at Fighting Island and Pelee Island turning out to be complete fiascos, Patriot leaders began to reassess their situation. During the spring and summer of 1838 a minimal amount of filibustering took place. Publicity and open organization were replaced by a new tactic of secrecy. The Patriots began to establish an underground organization. On March 19, 1838 in Lockport, New York, thirteen Patriot leaders including Dr. Alexander Mackenzie, General Donald McLeod and Dr. Charles Duncombe formed a committee to gather information about Canadian exiles in the United States. The Canadian Refugee Relief Association was further charged with the responsibility of formulating articles of association which would redress grievances and adopt measures conducive to their welfare. Dr. Mackenzie, formerly a Hamilton physician, was elected president. Agents were to be sent out with the purpose of establishing branch unions. General McLeod who had recently arrived from Ohio, was made "general organizer" by the committee.

Disturbances along the frontier were soon renewed, prompted by the efforts of the Association.[26] The burning of the steamer Sir Robert Peel at Well's Island, an abortive raid planned to be launched from Lewiston, New York, and the engagement at Short Hills ended the attempts of this group to orchestrate "independence" for the Canadas. William Lyon Mackenzie, while a member of the Association, distanced himself from its actions. He disapproved of the methods used and counselled the Lockport collaborative to abandon its efforts. Mackenzie noted that:

> Their organization and union apart from that of the associations who aid them, is nothing. They have little influence, nor will it increase until a better system is adopted. I shall try to get up such an organization -- and make such use of that already in operation, as will probably somewhat change the aspect of Canadian affairs. The material is before us if we choose to make use of it.[27]

What was the state of affairs and how much support did the Patriot cause still have in Upper Canada? Patriot sympathizer Linus W. Miller, made a tour through the province in the spring of 1838. His observations led him to surmise that spirits were still high and that the desire for rebellion had not been stamped out. Miller suggested that mismanagement and indecision on the part of Patriot leaders had resulted in past defeats. He concluded:

> I was universally assured that a large majority of the most respectable Canadians, were more anxious than ever for independence, and that the situation of the country alone prevented their effective organization.[28]

On the American side of the border preparations continued to be made for an invasion by a combined force of Canadian refugees and American supporters. Miller submitted that:

> Tens of thousands of the most respectable citizens of the northern States cheerfully and zealously gave their influence to the cause, and directly or indirectly encouraged the enterprise.[29]

Excitement and further support was increased with the execution of Samuel Lount and Peter Matthews on April 13, 1838.

In June, a new organization promoting revolution in Canada began recruiting members in Michigan. The Sons of Liberty set up headquarters in Detroit. General Henry S. Handy was again pressed into service and became commander in chief of troops associated with this movement. Agents were sent throughout the provinces to form secret lodges. Two hundred companies of one hundred men each were to be established during the month. Arms to equip this force were to be purloined from the Michigan state arsenal. Windsor was to be attacked on July 4. Accounts from several Patriots confirmed these plans. Linus Miller noted that for months extensive plans were made to invade Canada on that date. Precautions were taken to prevent disturbances along the border until then. Miller was sent by General McLeod in mid-June to bring back Patriots who had crossed into Canada to participate in the Short Hills raid.[30] Robert Marsh, who was involved in the battle of Pelee Island and who returned to Detroit during the summer of 1838, described the prevailing mood:

> Great preparations were being made all over the country for renewing the war. As many of our citizens were confined, and executions taking place in different parts of Canada, in the upper as well as the lower Province, and taunts and threats by tories were daily occurances, it was concluded best by many from Canada as well as thousands on this side to make one more trial.[31]

A brief Patriot landing on the Canadian shore of the St. Clair River on June 28, and numerous rumours of an impending July 4 strike, resulted in defensive action being taken.[32] Colonel John Prince ordered constables to seize and impound all boats and canoes and to check all passengers arriving at the local ferry landing. More British regulars were deployed throughout the province, and the size of the British naval fleet on Lake Erie was increased. On the American side, General Hugh Brady patrolled the Detroit River with armed vessels. His land forces were augmented by three additional companies from the 2nd U.S. artillery. American customs agents were ordered to prosecute anyone violating neutrality laws. This strict adherence to security resulted in little intercourse being permitted between Detroit and Windsor.[33]

General Henry S. Handy's plan to invade the Western District on July 4 collapsed when efforts to secure sufficient arms proved to be unsuccessful. The attempt of the Sons of Liberty to raise the "standard of revolt" in Essex County ended. All other Patriot organizations soon merged together with the Hunter's Lodge. The first of these lodges was apparently established in May of 1838. Followers swore to promote "republican institutions" and to rid North America of "all tyrants of Britain".[34] In addition, the function of this secret brotherhood was to collect and disburse funds to pay expenses, and to purchase provisions for the Patriot forces. The most important lodges were situated at Port Huron, Rochester, Buffalo, Cincinnati and Detroit. The grand lodge of the west was located at Cleveland. Estimates of membership ranged from 15,000 to 20,000. Contemporary reports suggested that support came from all walks of life for the Hunter's cause:

Labourers left their employ; apprentices their masters; mechanics abandoned their shops; merchants, their counters; husbands, their families; children, their parents; Christians, their churches; ministers of the gospel, their charge to attend these meetings.[35]

Between September 16 and 22, 1838, a convention of representatives from various lodges was held in Cleveland. Here a republican government for Upper Canada was formed. Lucius Versus Bierce, an Ohio lawyer, was made commander in chief of the reformed Patriot army. Plans for an extensive army and fleet along with the establishment of the "Republican Bank of Canada" were formulated. Preparations for invasion by the Hunters continued into the fall. Military excursions into Lower Canada and at Prescott were supported by the Hunters' Lodge, but again met with little success. A British traveller of the period recorded his thoughts about these incursions:

Under the plausible pretext of regeneration of Canada, it was apparent that an indiscriminate plunder of Canadians was contemplated.[36]

These events in the east increased tension in the Western District. While mid-October rumours of a planned attack on Fort Malden did not prove to be accurate, reports of Patriot forces training near Fort Gratoit resulted in the Essex militia being called out. To help maintain neutrality laws, General Brady chartered the steamer Illinois and continued to patrol the Detroit River. In late November the schooner Victory was captured by British troops aboard the steamer Lady. Several hundred stand of arms and a quantity of munitions and provisions were confiscated. The Victory was handed over to General Brady and the Detroit collector of customs, John McDonnel at Fort Malden. The Illinois then made for Detroit with her prize. John Prince's diary entry for November 19 echoed the prevailing atmosphere and noted preparations that were being undertaken:

Threatened attacks by Brigands from Michigan. Very much engaged all day in preparing. In the Evening placed a picket of my volunteers on duty, Patrol etc. Marched to the Ferry and was on duty all night. A bitter frost & cold indeed it was. No attack, but many threatened.[37]

In Cleveland, a Patriot regiment under command of Brigadier General Salathiel S. Coffinbury, received orders from General Handy to proceed to Detroit. There they were joined by rebel supporters from Buffalo, Rochester and other parts of Michigan. At one point, the encampment housed 600 men. Internal bickering by Patriot leaders and countermanding of orders resulted in widespread discontent among these troops. Over half of those assembled left ranks.[38] Rivalry for leadership between Generals Lucius Bierce and E.J. Roberts prompted further discord. Edward Theller who had recently escaped from captivity in Quebec, attempted to reach Detroit to provide some direction. His mission was to "prevent, by my presence and reasoning with the patriots...the utter folly and hopelessness of attempting an invasion of the western district at that time."[39] His efforts however were in vain.

Diligent patrols by the Brady Guards thwarted Patriot efforts to hijack a steamer on November 30 and December 1. A letter sent to General Brady by John Prince on December 1, noted the urgent situation that was at hand:

> I have ascertained from unquestionable authority that upwards of 1000 men left Buffalo a few days back in Steamers, and that they were to be reinforced all along the Shore of Lake Erie until they mustered about 5000 men; and that their determination is to make a descent upon Malden or some part of this frontier tonight. I have also this very afternoon been informed by one professing to be (but not being in reality) a "Patriot", that there is a camp no less than 400 of these Scoundrels in the woods about 2 miles back of Springwells; and that their fixed determination is to attack us here or at Windsor this night.[40]

On December 2, word was received at Sandwich that invasion was imminent. Defending forces were put on alert. The attack did not materialize as drifting ice apparently frustrated this attempt. The following evening, General Bierce and his followers marched through the streets of Detroit and took possession of the steamer Champlain. After some delay the rebel party crossed into Canadian waters early on the morning of December 4, and landed opposite the lower end of Belle Island. The invasion force of Canadian insurgents and American confederates was headed by General Bierce. His second in command was Canadian expatriate, General William Putnam. The rebel body numbered between 150-180, and was divided into two detachments under Colonels Harvell and Cunningham. A rearguard of 25 was commanded by Colonel Coffinbury. The Patriots had expected to be augmented by 500 additional Canadian sympathizers, but this support did not appear. Samuel Snow who had joined the Patriots in Cleveland, after hearing a rousing speech given by Dr. Charles Duncombe, noted the disappointing response:

> Not a Canadian met us on our arrival save a few who joined us in Michigan, and some of these turned traitor soon after.[41]

The rebels moved towards Windsor and came upon a guardhouse occupied by members of the Essex militia. After a "short but spirited resistance" by the Canadian defenders, the position was captured and the building burned. Nearby at Van Allen's wharf, the steamer _Thames_ was torched in reprisal for the burning of the _Caroline_. A company of Patriots commanded by General Putnam, advanced down Sandwich Street and encamped in an orchard behind the Francis Baby house. By 6 o'clock Windsor was in the hands of the rebel forces. An alarm was raised and companies of the provincial volunteer militia and the Essex militia responded. At 6:30 this force engaged the invaders. A "skirmishing fight" ensued. General Bierce did not attempt to assist his compatriots and could not be persuaded to advance to aid General Putnam's beseiged detachment. Bierce and Colonel Coffinbury retreated back to the safety of Detroit. Reinforcements that tried to cross the Detroit River were challenged by federal troops patrolling on the steamer _Erie_, and were turned back.

Enthusiasm for the success of the invasion was shown in Detroit where thousands were assembled to cheer on the Patriot forces.[42] Robert Marsh who was a lieutenant in General Putnam's brigade, noted the spectacle that he viewed across the river:

> There were thousands to be seen at day-light, on the tops of buildings swinging their hats and cheering us on our morning's success.[43]

Without additional military assistance forthcoming, General Putnam was compelled to order his forces to withdraw. Henry Grant, editor of the _Sandwich Western Herald_ described the scene that he witnessed at this juncture:

> The straggling volunteers of Sandwich, of whom we had the honor to constitute a part, came up in time to send a few leaden messengers after the fast-footed pirates, who fled with a velocity unexampled in the annals of locomotion.[44]

The Patriots were caught in a murderous crossfire and pandemonium reigned supreme as the rebels attempted escape.

By 8 a.m. the Patriots had been routed. Colonel John Prince sent the militia back to Sandwich to counter another rumoured attack. Several captives were ordered executed by Prince. Other escapers were arrested by American troops patrolling the Detroit River on three armed vessels. A number of the Patriots including General Putnam and Colonel Harvell were killed. The remainder of the invading force still left on Canadian soil, was tracked down by Indians and British regulars,[45] captured and jailed in Sandwich.

The Patriot army had been decimated. John Prince's diary account for December 4, provides chilling details of the event:

> Awoke at 6 a.m. by an alarm gun at Sandwich. Rose &
> saw a fire at Windsor. Proceeded there with the
> Militia & found it in possession of Brigands and
> Pirates. We attacked them & killed 27 and took 20
> Prisoners. I ordered the first 5 taken to be
> shot.[46]

On the following day the Patriot's vessel the <u>Champlain</u> was
seized by Detroit port collector John McDonnel. While the
controversy over Colonel Prince's executions was yet to be
heard, and captured rebels faced trials, imprisonment and
transportation, the Patriot army had for all purposes been
finally defeated and dispersed. The curtain had fallen on the
"last grand act" of the Patriot War!

One year after this attack the <u>Sandwich Western Herald</u>
assessed the existing state of affairs. An editorial noted
that:

> We heartily trust that a continuation of the peace
> at present so happily existing along our borders
> will make 'our folks' forget that anything so
> dreadful as the 'Battle of Windsor' ever happened at
> all![47]

Support for peaceful coexistence also came from Patriot
quarters. Edward Theller, who now published a newspaper in
Detroit, realized that the efforts of the Patriots to
"liberate" Upper Canada had failed. He claimed that the
Patriots and Canadians had reached a consensus and that, "We
have come to the conclusion not to go until <u>we</u> are wanted; and
<u>they</u> say when they want <u>us</u>, they will send."[48]

The events that took place in Essex County in 1838 cannot
be isolated from their larger context. The 1837 rebellions in
Upper and Lower Canada had been put down, but many supporters
of the cause had fled to the American border states to be
joined by U.S. sympathizers. Convinced that there would be
support for a popular uprising against British "Oppression and
Tyranny", the Patriot forces had attempted to "liberate" the
Canadian provinces through acts of armed aggression. Ignorant
of the real issues at hand, and lacking any official sanction,
Patriot forces attempted to overthrow the governments of the
Canadas against staggering odds. A comment in an 1839 issue
of the <u>Canadian Christian Examiner</u> outlined the misguided
motives associated with the Patriot cause:

> The grievances under which we were reported to be
> suffering awakened the sympathy of some, and the
> party divisions existing among us indicating
> weakness stimulated the rapacity of others. To
> these causes we may fairly ascribe the banding of
> multitudes on their frontier for the invasion of our

territory, or in their own language 'to assist the oppressed Canadians to gain their freedom.'[49]

Apart from deficiencies in military strength and poor leadership, Patriot forces never came to a full understanding of the difference in philosophies between American and British traditions. A strong sense of social conservatism and attachment to the British crown resulted in an exhibition of loyalty by the residents of Essex county. When challenged by a "republican onslaught", they became more steadfast in their monarchical preference and support.[50]

The successful repulsion of invading Patriot forces in the Western District brought the Rebellions of 1837-38 to an end.

Notes

1. Gourlay to Van Rensselaer, January 16, 1838, cited in John Charles Dent, The Story of the Upper Canadian Rebellion (Toronto, 1895), v. 2, p. 227.

2. For a thorough description of McLeod, see William Morley's introduction in Donald McLeod, A Brief Review of the Settlement in Upper Canada (Belleville, 1972), introduction.

3. Robert Marsh, Seven Years of My Life or a Narrative of a Patriot Exile (Buffalo, 1848), p. 7.

4. For additional information about Sutherland and other figures central to the Patriot cause, see Robert B. Ross, The Patriot Wars (Lansing, 1894), pp. 60 -88.

5. Edward A. Theller, Canada in 1837-38: Showing by Historical Facts, the Causes of the Late Attempted Revolution and Its Failure (Philadelphia, 1841), v. 1 p. 129.

6. R. Alan Douglas, ed., John Prince (Toronto, 1980), pp. 18-19.

7. Sutherland to Van Rensselaer, January 9, 1838, quoted in the Niles National Register (February 3, 1838), cited in Roger L. Rosentreter, "To Free Upper Canada: Michigan and the Patriot War, 1837-39", Phd. Dissertation, Michigan State University (1983), p. 75.

8. Theller, Revolution, v. 1, p. 136.

9. Orrin Edward Tiffany, The Canadian Rebellion of 1837-38 (Buffalo, 1905), p. 47.

10. W.W. Dodge to Thomas Sutherland, January 13, 1838 in the _Monroe Gazette_ (January 27, 1838), cited in Rosentreter, "Patriot War", p. 84.

11. _Ibid._, p. 98.

12. Tiffany, _Rebellion_, pp. 140-41.

13. McLeod, _Review_, p. 213.

14. Theller, _Revolution_, v. 1, p. 171.

15. Katherine M.J. McKenna, "The Impact of the Upper Canadian Rebellion on Life in Essex County, Ontario, 1837-42", unpublished research conducted for Parks Canada, Ontario Region, (1985), p. 58.

16. _Ibid._, p. 58.

17. Tiffany, _Rebellion_, pp. 140-41.

18. Rosentreter, "Patriot War", p. 105.

19. Ashley to Bond, Lower Sandusky, March 1, 1838, cited in Tiffany, _Rebellion_, p. 142.

20. McLeod, _Review_, p. 216.

21. Douglas, _Prince_, p. 20.

22. J.P. Martyn, "The Patriot Invasion of Pelee Island", _Ontario History_, (September 1964), pp. 158-59.

23. McLeod, _Review_, p. 220.

24. Maitland to Foster, March 4, 1838, printed in the _New York Albion_, (March 17, 1838).

25. Tiffany, _Rebellion_, p. 145.

26. _Ibid._, p. 54.

27. Charles Lindsey, _The Life and Times of William Lyon Mackenzie_, (Toronto, 1862), v. 2, p. 232.

28. Linus W. Miller, _Notes of an Exile to Van Dieman's Land_, (Fredonia, N.Y., 1846), p. 3.

29. _Ibid._

30. _Ibid._, p. 17.

31. Marsh, _Seven Years_, p. 19.

32. R. Alan Douglas, "The Battle of Windsor", _Ontario History_, (September 1969), p. 139.

33. Theller, _Revolution_, v. 2, p. 312.

34. Tiffany, _Rebellion_, p. 62.

35. _Report of the Select Committee of Upper Canada, April 30, 1839_, cited in _Ibid._, p. 63.

36. T.R. Preston, _Three Years' Residence in Canada From 1837-1839_, (London, 1840), v. 1, p. 154.

37. Douglas, _Prince_, p. 25.

38. Ross, _Patriot War_, p. 45.

39. Theller, _Revolution_, v. 2, p. 294.

40. Douglas, _Prince_, p. 26.

41. Samuel Snow, _The Exile's Return, or Narrative of Samuel Snow_, (Cleveland, 1846), p. 3.

42. Preston, _Residence_, v. 1, p. 172.

43. Marsh, _Exile_, p. 22.

44. Douglas, "Battle", p. 142.

45. For a first hand accout see, Snow, _Exile's_, pp. 3-5.

46. Douglas, _Prince_, p. 26.

47. Roger Rosentreter, "The Patriot War in Michigan", unpublished paper, Michigan Department of State, (Spring, 1987), p. 25.

48. Theller, _Ibid._

49. Fred Landon, _An Exile From Canada_, (Toronto, 1960), p. 100.

50. McKenna, "Impact", p. 249.

Links between Upper and Lower Canada, 1837-1838: The Well-Affected and the Disaffected

Elinor Kyte Senior

In discussing the rebellions of 1837 and 1838 it is important to emphasize the distinction between Reformer and Rebel and between Patriote and Insurgent. The terms are by no means synonymous. In Lower Canada the Reformers took the name Patriotes and in both provinces the vast majority of Reformers did not become Rebels. As the Indian warrior of Caughnawaga, Georges de Lorimier, adamantly declared, "I am a Patriote; but I am no Rebel".[1] Rebels in both provinces were a militant minority wing of the Reformers.

A second point, again an obvious one but one that must be emphasized, is that rebellion is open, armed and organized resistance to an established government. Its objective is to overthrow that government by force. That is why every government regards rebellion and its twin sister -- treason-- as the most heinous of crimes, punishable usually by death. Every country will use its security forces to the utmost to suppress rebellion. Otherwise, the successful rebels are revolutionary leaders of a newly-established government which faces a dilemma: to reverence its revolutionary leaders but never imitate their method of gaining power.

In Lower Canada in 1837 the majority of the population would probably have identified themselves as reform, whig or independent, rather than tory. This included many of the English community. In Upper Canada Reformers had lost out in the political arena in 1836, whether by fair or foul means, but by 1837 pro-government forces were in the ascendancy in the Assembly and these included many Reformers such as Egerton Ryerson.

If we look for links between Upper and Lower Canadian Reformers prior to the rebellions, there are many. William Lyon Mackenzie spent time in Montreal before he, like most immigrants, moved on to greener fields in Upper Canada. His association with Reformers in the lower province dated back to 1831 when he travelled to Quebec City to see the Assembly in action. There he met Louis-Joseph Papineau, leader of the Patriote Party and Speaker of the Assembly, with whose "frank, affable and candid manners" he was much pleased.[2] But three years later when Reformer John Neilson, editor of the <u>Quebec Gazette</u>, broke with Papineau over the issue of the 92 Resolutions, Mackenzie was dismayed. "Divided as you now are," he wrote to Neilson, "the spirit of the people may be broken down for years". Mackenzie's own disillusionment with Papineau burst out a year later. Mackenzie was furious that the Lower Canadian Assembly had deprived Neilson of the government printing "because a Canadian stept in to do the work a trifle cheaper".[3]

To Dr. Edmund P. O'Callaghan, the Irish editor of Papineau's English-langauge newspaper, the <u>Vindicator</u>, Mackenzie wrote, "I am fearful this national origin business was the guiding principle. You were under immense obligation of Neilson. He has stood by the Canadians like a rock". Mackenzie told O'Callaghan that he would continue to support Papineau publicly. "Not one whisper shall be heard either from Dr. O'Grady or myself on matters like these beyond the circle of those who already know them. How my head ached when you told me Papineau had grudged us the pittance of printing. Mr. Papineau will be civil to us, but nothing more."[4]

Thus by 1835 Mackenzie privately considered that whatever liaison the Upper Canadian Reformers would have with the Patriots under Papineau, it would be one of convenience rather than of principle. It is not surprising, then, that he somewhat pompously informed Neilson, "These are not the days when changes of government are produced in America by violence and brute force".[5] Ironically, two years later, Mackenzie would resort to violence and brute force, when Papineau found himself almost buffeted into rebellion by forces which he had aroused but no longer controlled.

As the undisputed leader of Lower Canada, Papineau looked to men like Robert Baldwin, Dr. John Rolph and Marshall Spring Bidwell, Speaker of the Upper Canadian Assembly, as his social and political equals, rather than to Mackenzie. Still, Papineau wrote to Mackenzie frequently, as he did to Bidwell, Baldwin and other Reformers, so much so that Dr. Thomas Daniel Morrison of Toronto cautioned Papineau against Mackenzie in 1835.[6] This was at a time when Reformers of both provinces began to suspect, and with reason, that their letters were being tampered with at the Post Office. They made arrangements to exchange mail under cover of the Toronto Reformer and brewer, John Doel. In spite of these precautions, Papineau still feared that his mail was being delayed and examined. In 1836 he urged Bidwell to consider a personal meeting where they could work out a common programme. Papineau's special concern was the Legislative Council which he wanted made elective. He scolded the Upper Canadian Reformers for concentrating too much on a reform of the Executive Council.[7]

With Mackenzie's political defeat in 1836 and the loss of his power base as Mayor of Toronto, he opted for a new newspaper, The Constitution, and he re-organized the Toronto Alliance Society into a political union. Boldly on 19 July 1837 he described how the political unions, with branches of young men in most reform centres, could be easily transformed into a para-military unit.[8] Scarcely a month later Montreal Patriotes organized a similar youth section, the Sons of Freedom, with a civilian front easily convertible to military units. Their immediate model was the Van Kleek Hill Sons of Liberty, already in existence in that Ottawa Valley centre of reform agitation.[9] This is just one example of the way the militant Reformers in both provinces imitated or influenced each other in the months prior to the outbreak of armed revolt.

Late in July of 1837 Mackenzie met with other Reformers at Doel's brewery in Toronto to write a Declaration of Rights and Grievances, modelled on the American Declaration of Independence, and made plans for a "Convention of the Peoples of the Two Canadas". Throughout these summer months of 1837, then, Mackenzie openly planned and sought cooperation with Papineau. At subsequent meetings, solidarity with the Patriotes of Lower Canada was a common theme with frequent expressions of sympathy for "Mr. Papineau and the brave and patriotic inhabitants of Lower Canada whose liberties are threatened".[10]

As political positions became polarized in both provinces and as the more prudent or the more frightened Reformers drew away from Mackenzie and Papineau, the two leaders may have felt more in need of each other's support. The dependence, however, was greater on the part of Mackenzie. He could count neither on the neutrality of the greater part of the people, as Papineau could, nor rely on the commitment of his own forces. Thus Mackenzie anxiously watched each move of the Lower Canadian Patriotes towards extreme measures, and used such moves to bolster his hesitant colleagues who, by October of 1837, were toying with the idea of physical force to gain political ends.

The lieutenant-governor of Upper Canada, Sir Francis Bond Head, thought that Mackenzie's agitation was primarily designed to draw troops away from the Lower Provinces and thus give Papineau's forces a free hand. Ironically, the intensity of agitation in the lower province resulted in troops being sent there from the upper province. In fact, it was the removal of the last three companies of the 24th Regiment from Toronto on 30 October 1837 that was seized upon by Mackenzie to convince his colleagues that armed resistance was at last a possibility -- that the province was defenceless.

As soon as the regulars embarked from the Queen's Wharf in Toronto for the lower province, Mackenzie urged immediate action. But his country supporters hung back. They wanted assurance that the Lower Canadians and the Toronto Reformers meant business. To satisfy all, Mackenzie agreed to send an agent to the lower province. The top brass, Doctors John Rolph and Thomas Morrison, both refused to go.[11] The task fell to the wealthy Quaker farmer, Jesse Lloyd of Lloydtown. Armed with a personal introduction to O'Callagahan from Dr. Morrison and other letters from Dr. Rolph and Mackenzie, Lloyd reached Montreal the first weekend of November at the precise time that the first street skirmish took place between the Sons of Liberty and the Montreal Constitutionalists. Lloyd sought out Thomas Storrow Brown, the bankrupt hardware merchant who had been elected general of the military wing of the Montreal Sons of Liberty.

With an air of injured innocence or perhaps with tongue-in-cheek, Brown recalled this meeting with Lloyd many years later. "So general was the idea abroad that we were organized and ripe for revolt," he wrote, "that Mackenzie, who planned a rising in Toronto and an attack upon the capital, sent an agent to communicate his designs and to learn ours".[12] With great secrecy Lloyd visited Papineau who summoned O'Callaghan and Dr. Robert Nelson for a conference. Lloyd returned to Toronto with word that "there would be no drawing back of Lower Canada - that it was deemed proper to defer the movement till the ice began to form on the St. Lawrence, when there would be no crossing of troops, that our prompt cooperation agreeable to our public pledge, was confidentially reckoned upon in all their calculations and that Mr. Papineau would send a messenger to Dr. Rolph, myself and others, warning us when to move".[13]

It was the receipt of Lloyd's news from Lower Canada that spurred the hesitant in Upper Canada. Mackenzie met with Dr. John Rolph and Dr. Thomas Morrison immediately to discuss the "propriety of an immediate revolution or any at all". Morrison confessed later that "Dr. Rolph and myself, having much doubt as to whether the people were desirous of it or would engage in it, Mr. Mackenzie strenuously opposed our views, by insisting that the people desired it and that forthwith. He assured us he had lists, signed by some thousands, for the avowed purpose, and upbraided us very vehemently for forsaking the people, if we did not go with them in their wishes, which were to depose the Government and establish our own, especially under so favourable a crisis, there being no troops left in the garrison".[14]

Morrison admitted the Reformers "consented that Mackenzie might proceed into the country, and consult with the different political unions on this important subject, and bring it to their decision. If they were for a revolution, and willing to effect it; and when he had done so to inform us of the result. We then also laid down a plan by which we might take possession of the arms, and put into custody the different officers of Government, and establish a Provisional Government".[15]

Morrison's admissions show that the Upper Canadian attempt at rebellion was not entirely Mackenzie's decision, though he was the prime mover.

Thus, from early November 1837, there were definite plans and preparations afoot in both provinces, with mutually-agreed timing and communications to be established between the upper and lower Canadian conspirators. When Papineau secretly quit Montreal on 13 November for the Richelieu Valley, several days before the government issued warrants for the arrests of the Patriote chiefs, he sent his messenger, Theophile Dufort, a Patriote magistrate, to Mackenzie to "begin the day in the upper province in order", as Mackenzie said, "to assist the Lower Canadians in their struggle for independence".[16]

In other words, the Upper Canadian rising had something of a diversionary character about it. That such pre-arranged plans had been made between conspirators in both provinces is certain. There is not only the evidence from Mackenzie's later published accounts, parts of which are questionable, but there is also a confidential letter written by Mackenzie in exile to his fellow exile, Dr. E.B. O'Callaghan. In this private letter Mackenzie in 1844 ruminates cynically about the post-rebellion government posts given to former Lower Canadian Patriots. He reminded O'Callaghan that "when yourself and friends sent up...to Toronto in November 1837 to urge us to rise against the British government, it certainly would not have come into my thoughts that the men who did that would, in the event of failure, make a treaty with England for the patronage of Canada to themselves and our tory enemies, and forget that I had an existence".[17] Had no agent been sent from Lower Canada, Mackenzie would not have mentioned it so matter-of-factly in a private letter to O'Callaghan who was in a position to know whether Mackenzie was lying. Nor would Mackenzie have reminded O'Callaghan that "When your trouble began on the 6th of Nov. 1837 we were in quietness in Toronto. When we moved 5th Dec. the game was up with you, and the history of your failures spread thro' Upper Canada in the gazettes. I had pledged myself that no change of circumstances would make me untrue to you, and faithfully and at the greatest risque did I redeem that pledge".[18]

Thus there existed close links between the leaders of the militant radicals in each province in the fall of 1837 and pre-arranged plans for simultaneous uprisings. The other side of the coin were the links at governmental levels between the two provinces and the collaboration of military forces from the Eastern District of Upper Canada with those in the lower province. Just as Reformers-turned-Rebels had made mutually-convenient plans for help when rebellion broke out, so, too, did government and military forces. Sir Francis Head's action in sending all the regulars to Lower Canada had been mutually agreed upon as early as 24 October 1837, a week previously.[19] There was nothing rash about his action. What Head would not do, however, was to allow Upper Canadian militiamen to cross the provincial border. It was not until after Sir John Colborne, the commander of the British forces, had suppressed insurgencies in the Richelieu Valley and the Lake of the Two Mountains, that the men of Glengarry received permission from Head to march to the lower province.[20] Part of Head's reluctance sprang from his fear that radical Reformers in the Eastern District might make trouble.

Colborne already had alarming reports about this District from his somewhat alarmist intelligence officer at Cornwall, Royal Engineer Captain George Phillpotts, a personal friend. Phillpotts warned Colborne of disaffection among the St. Regis Indians, located opposite Cornwall, and of terror among Irish and Scottish settlers near Dundee who feared that they would lose their lands if they did not join the Patriotes. What was even more surprising, Phillpotts feared that the Roman Catholic Glengarries would not fight against their co-religionists in the lower province.[21]

"The Protestants", he wrote to Colborne, "are, I believe, all loyal, but I have heard that the R. Catholics are determined not to act against..the R(oman) Catholics of Lower Canada... They say, or at least some of them say, that they look upon it not in a Political point of view, but that their Religion is in danger. To this it was replied that the Bishop's letter, lately published, ought to satisfy them... when it was ans(were)d that the B(ishop) rec(eive)d a salary and was in some measure depend(ent) on Gov(ernment),... that they knew well if the Gov(ernment) succeeds in putting down Papineau, the next step will be to put down the R(oman) Catholic religion."[22]

Radical Reform elements did exist at St. Andrew's, above Cornwall, at Lochiel, and at Van Kleek Hill and other centres including Cornwall, but Phillpotts thought these elements would be ashamed to hang back once Glengarry and Stormont militia regiments were mobilized. Phillpotts soon modified his views about the possible disaffection in the Eastern District and assured Colborne that he could count on both the Indians and the Glengarries.[23] However, it was Phillpotts' initial alarmist views from an area Colborne thought was staunchly loyal that may have prompted Colborne to act as precipitously as he did in the first military moves against the insurgents in the Richelieu Valley.

Though tied to Toronto politically, the Eastern District was linked to Montreal geographically, commercially and fraternally. One British officer, the man who would lead the successful attack against St. Charles on 25 November 1837, had no qualms whatever about the Eastern District. Colonel George Wetherall of the 1st Royal Scots remarked somewhat smugly on the eve of the first skirmish in Montreal, "All Glengarry is anxious to join us in suppressing any insurrection in the Lake of the Two Mountains."[24]

Wetherall was right. The moment radicalism turned to armed, organized and open resistance to the established government, the officers of the four Glengarry Regiments drew up a statement of unqualified loyalty to the Crown and published it in the Montreal _Transcript_.[25] Another writer from Glengarry assured Montrealers that "both Catholic and protestant Highlanders are ready to turn out, even those we used to call Radicals... They say that although they were and are radical for reform, they will never fight against Britain."[26] Only one regiment held back for a time -- the 1st Stormont, commanded by Donald Aeneas Macdonell, the Reform member for the County. He hesitated to call a meeting of his officers for fear the more radical members of the regiments would hang back.[27]

The men of Cornwall and Glengarry were soon put to the test for on 2 December 1837 they got an urgent request from Colonel John Simpson, the collector of customs at Coteau-du-Lac just over the line in the lower province. Simpson was a Reformer and a close personal friend of Papineau. But when he learned that insurgents were planning to seize the customs fort at Coteau-du-Lac, he hastily conveyed the cannon and shot from the fort and sank it in the St. Lawrence to avoid its capture by the insurgents.[28] Then he rounded up all the loyalists he could in the area and posted them in the fort day and night. When news reached him that more insurgents were on their way from Vaudreuil to attack the fort, Simpson sent a plea to Cornwall for help.

The response was immediate. Colonel Philip Vankoughnet sent fifty armed Cornwall volunteers off under Captain Benjamin French.[29] The Indians of St. Regis lent their ceremonial field piece to the Cornwall detachment and provided some barrels of pork, an earnest indication of their good feelings towards government. This was an unexpected development as far as the radicals in the border zone were concerned. The arrival of militiamen from the upper province perturbed them considerably for they had believed their own propaganda that the upper province was more ready for revolt than their own. Merchant William Whitlock of Vaudreuil, who had made no secret of his admiration for American institutions, had been publishing such inflammatory pamphlets attacking the government that Vaudreuil Patriotes assumed that the English and Scots in nearby Glengarry and Stormont were also disenchanted with government.[30]

Men like the Vaudreuil merchants, Francois-Xavier Desjardins and his brother, Fabien, and their cousin, Alselme, took the lead in the agitation against government, but once it was realized that Glengarry and Cornwall men were prepared to garrison Coteau-du-Lac, their plans to seize other vital points in this area such as the Cedars, Cascades, and Pointe Claire, were abandoned.[31]

Once fighting broke out in the lower province, the martial spirit in Glengarry and Stormont knew no bounds. Now Phillpotts informed Colborne that the great fear was that "you will quiet the rebels without assistance" from Glengarry.[32] Part of this martial enthusiasm stemmed from the threats that the Glengarries were now receiving from the radicals across the provincial line. Patriots in Vaudreuil and Rigaud warned that if the Glengarries should march to Lower Canada the Canadians of Rigaud would destroy their farms while they were away.[33] Thus the initial events at the outbreak in Lower Canada saw polarization on the Eastern District border zone where just a few weeks earlier there had been expressions of solidarity between the Catholics of the Eastern District and those in Lower Canada. This polarization would remain as one of the legacies in this area after the rebellion, for the Glengarries did cross the border, not in time to aid Colborne in the Lake of the Two Mountains, but as soon as Mackenzie's abortive uprising fizzled out, Sir Francis Head gave the green light for Upper Canadian volunteers to march to Lower Canada.

Two regiments of Glengarries were ordered to the neighbouring province in the spring of 1838 after exiled insurgents made several raids into the province from the American side. The job of the Glengarries was to police the area south of the St. Lawrence and keep an eye on disaffected elements.[34] With the arrival of large numbers of regular reinforcements from Great Britain in May 1838, the Glengarries were demobilized and returned home. During the summer Sir James Macdonell, brother of the late Highland chief, Glengarry, arrived in Quebec City with a brigade of guards. He lost no time in visiting Glengarry, in company with his kinsman, the first Catholic bishop of Upper Canada, Alexander Macdonell. Here he addressed the four Glengarry regiments in Gaelic, saying that he looked for a welcome, "not on my own account, but for the sake of my departed brother who, when in life, loved you more than life itself. You have proved by your past conduct... your warm and unshakable attachment to your Sovereign and the Constitution... should circumstances again call for your active services, I know you will uphold the character you have already established".[35]

It is not surprising, then, that when the second uprising broke out in Lower Canada three months later, Colborne had a body of loyal men from the Eastern District clamouring to serve under the brother of their late chieftain, and he left it to the Glengarry Regiments to surround the insurgents at Beauharnois. Additional pleas for help reached Cornwall from the Huntingdon Volunteers who had moved on a rebel encampment at Baker's Farm on the Chateauguay River. The first to offer his regiment for service in the lower province was Colonel Donald Aeneas Macdonell of the 1st Stormont, a mute testimony that events over the year had wiped away any fears that lingering Reform sentiment in the regiment would hinder its willingness to serve. The Stormont Highlanders immediately boarded vessels to cross the St. Lawrence to Dundee where fifty Indian warriors from St. Regis joined them in their march down the Chateauguay River to reinforce the Huntingdon Volunteers.[36]

With the march of some 1,400 Glengarry and Cornwall men on Beauharnois and down the Chateauguay River, the insurgents on the border realized all too well that there would be increasing fears that "the Scotch with the Indians are coming to massacre us", as one of them, himself part-Scots, candidly admitted at the subsequent court martial.[37]

This movement of the militia units from the Eastern District gave a new dimension to relations between the peoples near the provincial boundary. Hitherto there had been a growing rapport between Roman Catholic Scots and French Canadian co-religionists.[38] As well, there had been considerable political sympathy between Reformers in both areas. This was best personified by the fact that the leading rebel in Montreal in 1838 was John Macdonell, a son of a retired half-pay Scottish officer from St. Andrew's who had married into the prominent French Canadian de Belestre family.[39]

The rebellions of 1837-38 put a damper on this merging of the two communities. The people of the Eastern District of Upper Canada rallied to the government, coming well within the "loyalist" orbit. They assumed something of the anti-French attitude of that section of the Anglophone community of Montreal that now tended to regard all French Canada as disaffected.

Their attitude was expressed by the powerful Roman Catholic Bishop Alexander Macdonell. The year following the rebellions he came to Cornwall to preach what turned out to be his last sermon in Canada. Taking as his text, "Render unto Caesar the things that are Caesar's and unto God the things that are God's", he summed up his analysis of the rebellion in the neighbouring province. "The Canadians had no real grievances to complain of," he insisted. "They paid no tythes but to their own clergy; no taxes or other burthen but what was imposed upon them by laws of their own making; their religion was not only free and uncontrolled, but encouraged and protected by Government. In a word, "he declared, the French Canadians lived freer, more comfortably and more independently than any other class of subjects perhaps on the whole surface of the globe, until the folly and madness of Irreligious Papineau, Atheistical Girod, and Camelion O'Callaghan, of the Protestant Nelson, Browns and Scotts, and others of that kidney, made them believe that they were groaning under a galling yoke."[40]

The bitterness of the rebellion period lingered on in the Eastern District where Bishop Macdonell's stinging indictment of the leaders of the revolt stuck in memories. Thus the Catholics and others of the Eastern District regarded with some suspicion those few intrepid French Canadians who moved towards their boundaries in the immediate post-rebellion era and it may well have been this rupture in fraternal relations that explains the very small number of French Canadians who moved into the Eastern District prior to 1850.

Notes

1. Depositions of Georges de Lorimier (15 February, 1838) in Archives nationales de Quebec: Documents relatifs aux envenements de 1837-38, #2409.

2. Mackenzie to Neilson, (9 April, 1831), Public Archives of Ontario (PAO): Mackenzie-Lindsey Papers.

3. Ibid., (7 February, 1834 and 28 December, 1835).

4. Mackenzie to O'Callaghan, (25 November, 1835), in The Statesman, (Brockville, 27 August, 1837).

5. Mackenzie to Neilson, (28 December, 1835).

6. T.D. Morrison to Papineau, (20 April, 1835) in PAC: Papineau Papers, MG24/B2, ii., pp. 1939-42.

7. Papineau to Bidwell, (16 April, 1836), Ibid., p. 2162.

8. The Constitution, (Toronto, 19 July, 1837).

9. North American, (Swanton, Vt., 24 March, 1841).

10. Constitution, (Toronto, 26 July, 1837).

11. T.D. Morrison's station, (c. 1847), in J.C. Dent, Upper Canadian Rebellion, ii., p. 21.

12. T.S. Brown, "1837 and My Connection With It", in Dominion Monthly, (Montreal, April 1869), vol. 4, no. 1, p. 8.

13. For Lloyd's mission, see T.D. Morrison's statement in J.C. Dent, <u>Upper Canada Rebellion</u>, vol. 1, pp. 378, 383, and vol. 2, pp. 20-21; W.L. Mackenzie, "A Winter's Journey through the Canadas", in <u>The Tribune</u>, (New York, 28 April, 1849).

14. Morrison's statement, (c. 1847), in Dent, <u>Upper Canadian Rebellion</u>, ii., p. 21.

15. <u>Ibid</u>.

16. Mackenzie, "A Winter's Journey through the Canadas", <u>New York Tribune</u>, (28 April, 1849), see PAC: MG 24/B18/iv/169.

17. Mackenzie to O'Callaghan, (16 September, 1844), PAC: O'Callaghan Papers, MG24/B50, i.

18. <u>Ibid</u>.

19. Head to Colborne, (24 October, 1837), PAC: RG8/C1272; see also Head to Colborne, (31 October, 1837), PAC: Colborne Papers, MG24/A40, p. 2807.

20. Elinor Kyte Senior, <u>Redcoats & Patriotes: the Rebellions in Lower Canada 1837-38</u>, (Stittsville, 1985), p. 104.

21. Phillpotts to Colborne, (17 and 20 November, 1837), PAC: Colborne Papers, MG24/A40, pp. 2952-55.

22. See pastoral letter of Bishop J.J. Lartigue, Roman Catholic Bishop of Montreal, admonishing against agitation and insurrection, <u>Missiskoui Standard</u>, (Frelighsburg, 21 November, 1837), reprinted from <u>Montreal Weekly Herald</u>; see also Phillpotts to Colborne, (20 November, 1837), PAC: Colborne Papers, MG24/A40, pp. 2969-71.

23. Phillpotts to Colborne, (4 December, 1837), <u>Ibid</u>., pp. 3072, 3111.

24. Wetherall to Gosford, (6 November, 1837), PAC: Q239, p. 372.

25. <u>Transcript</u>, (Montreal, 2 December, 1837).

26. <u>Ibid</u>.

27. Phillpotts to Colborne, (4 December, 1837), PAC: Colborne Papers, MG24/A40, p. 3072.

28. <u>Gazette</u>, (Montreal, 9 December, 1837); see also Robert Ogle Gowan, "Memoirs of the Rebellions", in PAC: Ferguson Papers, MG27/IE30/v/19.

29. <u>Gazette</u>, (Montreal, 9 December, 1837).

30. M. Bellavance and G. Goyer, "Francois-Xavier Desjardins", <u>Dictionary of Canadian Biography</u>, ix, p. 203.

31. Robert Lionel Seguin, <u>Le Moouvement insurrectionel dans la Presqu'ile de Vaudreuil 1837-38</u>, (Montreal, 1955), p. 59.

32. Phillpotts to Colborne, (4 December, 1837), PAC: Colborne Papers, MG24/A40, p. 3111.

33. <u>Ibid</u>.

34. Colborne to Head, (3 February, 1838), PAC: RG8/C1272/84-5.

35. <u>Transcript</u>, (Montreal, 7 August, 1838).

36. Senior, <u>Redcoats & Patriotes</u>, pp. 187-8.

37. Pierre Reid's testimony in <u>Report of State Trials held before a General Court Martial 1838-39</u>, (Montreal, 1839), i, p. 42.

38. Elinor Kyte Senior, <u>From Royal Township to Industrial City: Cornwall 1784-1984</u>, (Belleville, 1983), pp. 134-147.

39. PAC: Audet Papers, vol. 20, p. 660; and PAC: RG4/A1/31/9911.

40. Extract of Bishop Macdonell's sermon are found in John Alexander Macdonnel, <u>Sketches of Glengarry in Canada</u>, (Montreal, 1893), pp. 267-277.

Rebellion Opposed

Why Not an Aristrocracy?

Anthony Adamson

> Let Every Person be subject to governing authorities. For there is no authority except from God, and those that exist have been instituted by God. Therefore he who resists authority resists what God has appointed, and those who resist will incur judgment.
>
> Romans 13:1

When this text was delivered from the lectern by Archdeacon Strachan at St. James Church in Toronto, the aristocratic people in the front pews hoped that the common people at the back would take heed. When, in his Bible readings, William Lyon Mackenzie came upon this text, I think he pondered. Was Paul, with his Roman passport, a compromiser? Or did Paul just worry that resistance in Rome then meant getting eaten by lions? In Upper Canada in the 1830s there were no lions, just a clutch of co-operating families on the make. They were on the make because they, or their parents, had all been losers at home, either in the United Kingdom or the United States. Mackenzie was the lion.

Had the title of this essay, "Why not an aristocracy?", been put as a question to Ontario's patron saint -- Upper Canada's first Lieutenant-Governor John Graves Simcoe, he would have replied, "how else can you run a country except with educated people of means, who have the time to devote to government, and who have a financial stake in the country?" Without an aristocracy and a squirearchy he saw the Terror of the Paris communes, or the chaos and injustice which was already quite evident to him in the Great Republic. It was also quite evident to Simcoe that the best system of government in the world was British.

Sir John Beverley Robinson wrote Lord Normanby after the rebellion to remind him that "there is no counteracting influence of an ancient Aristocracy, of a great landed interest or even a wealthy agricultural class...to stand between almost universal suffrage and those institutions which proudly and happily distinguish Britons." The counter-revolutionary influences lacking in Upper Canada included an established church. Elizabeth Simcoe, the wife of our patron saint, was so keen on the aristocracy that she prevented her daughters from marrying anybody and the Simcoe line died out. Not so the fate of the family of the individual who until recently was regarded as Upper Canada's great Satan. Some years ago I was asked to dinner in London to meet a man who had something to do with Canadian history, so I was told. I was introduced to, and at dinner sat next to Sir Francis Bond Head. He was proud of his forebear. The head of the Heads in each generation since, he said, was baptised Francis Head.

If I have any right to be discussing the rebellion it is because I have had a reasonably successful career in the inheriting business, which allows me to interpret history by extra-sensory perception. For example, I inherited the umbrella stand of Bishop Strachan. It stands by my front door and every day it has a message for me, the one from Romans 13. It used to be a little upset when my wife started to keep her golf clubs in it. But when I told it that I had married a descendent of two families that co-operated so well with each other, the Boultons and Robinsons, it has accepted her clubs. It is not only from Bishop Strachan's umbrella stand that I draw my perception of the need, or lack of any need for an aristocracy. My inheritance includes the documentary detritus of two great grandfathers, one of whom came over before Lord Durham to act as his spy. The other came over for Lord Normanby and Lord Sydenham to Toronto with the covert intention of setting up an established church. On top of all this I was born in Toronto at the corner of D'Arcy and Beverley Street, D'Arcy after Boulton, Beverley after Robinson, and when I went out in my pram I was once bumped by a rude man who had come to visit his mother who lived on the other or wrong side of Beverley Street -- William Lyon Mackenzie King. These documentary, material and environmental influences have of course not left me in any way biased. My own blood runs with the genes of a family of Reformers -- the Cawthras.

In this paper I propose to consider the attitudes of two families in the 1830s. The five aristocratic Boultons who Mackenzie put at the head of what he called the Family Compact and the Cawthras who were Reformers and not aristocratic.

The Boultons have already been adequately exposed for damnation by Mackenzie. D'Arcy senior, the immigrant, came of good landed gentry stock in Lincolnshire and had a wife whose family were leading legal lights in London. D'Arcy, being the third son, lost out in inheritance, so he articled for a year in a legal firm, and then did a most ungentlemanly thing -- he started a wool business. This went bust. He had to immigrate to the States in 1797, with his wife and a sizeable family where they lived a degrading life until he came north. In a book he wrote for colonists he said that when he crossed the St. Lawrence at Cornwall he "seemed at once to step home". He landed in a hive of Loyalists there. As he had a little bit of legal training, he decided to go where power rested -- the town of York. He did this in 1803 which happened to be the same year that Joseph Cawthra arrived there.

Lieutenant-Governor Simcoe had wanted to set up a Canadian aristocracy as soon as possible, and D'Arcy was pleased to supply himself and family to Simcoe's successor, Lieutenant-Governor Peter Hunter. Hunter was thereupon pleased to deem D'Arcy one of six "fit and proper to practice law in the Province due to their probity, education and condition in life." By 1805 he was solicitor-general or head policeman (salary £100 currency) and head of the new Law Society of Upper Canada (status and power). He scrambled after preferment, became attorney-general (£300 currency) and eventually became Mr. Justice Boulton (£750 currency) and died in 1834. His scrambling kept him busy crossing the Atlantic to press his case or to complain, just as Mackenzie did. In 1810 he was captured by a French privateer and interned at Verdun till 1813 on half pay. Except for this latter incident the same story may be told of four of his sons. D'Arcy junior married Sarah Robinson, built the Grange and died in 1846. Henry John married Miss Jones, sister of Lady MacNab, and built Holland House on the site of the present Royal York Hotel. George Strand went to Cobourg to start a well housed dynasty there. James went to Perth and built a replica of the Toronto Grange. There were also two sons, Charles and William, who died before Mackenzie could damn them, and there were two sisters who died as children.

The Boultons were probably less proud of their lineage than was the clan-conscious Mackenzie. William Lyon Mackenzie regarded the Boultons not as aristocrats but rather as bloodsuckers, men who made their way up in the world by being pleasant,"fawning and crying in the right circles". Upper Canadians wanted to behave like Americans but remain loyally British to that mythical holy grail "the Crown". If the great Satan, Sir Francis Bond Head, had not loused things up, and if the aristocratic Robinsons had just once asked the Mackenzies to dinner, perhaps the rebellion might never have taken place. Even so Mackenzie succeeded in obtaining justice almost as many times as he was rebuffed. He managed to have a Boulton, a Hagerman and Lieutenant-Governor Colborne fired by Lord Goderich. He was awarded £625 compensation for his printing press -- more than enough to set him up again. He was loved and admired by thousands. He is recognized in history as the first mayor of Toronto in 1834 (but nobody remembers that the chairman of petty sessions of the peace doing the same job for nothing during the cholera epidemic in 1833 was a Boulton). He was presented with a beautiful gold medal worth £250. He had a fine house with five bedrooms at one time in the 1830s. He spent nearly a year in England hob-nobbing with the peerage and was in the gallery of the House of Lords for the passing of the 1832 Reform Bill.

Mackenzie believed that to draw rulers from an upper class was an abomination, yet according to a number of historians his Reform assembly of 1828 was petty, confused and squabbled as futilely as any Tory assembly. Given an election contest in 1837 when "the people" (which to him meant the farmers) had the opportunity democratically to take over the assembly, "the people" voted for the great Satan, Sir Francis Bond Head. Beaten at the polls, Mackenzie organized his "contras" and managed to have the country almost invaded again by neighbouring, dangerously leftist proto-communists in the United States.

May I now go back to 1802 and consider a rowboat load of "boat people" pushing their way through the rushes along the front of York off a schooner which had brought them from Oswego. They were Joseph Cawthra, his wife Mary Turnpenny, his daughter Grace, aged 20, his sons John, Jonathan, and Henry (who had been kicked on the head by a horse) and baby William aged one year. Joseph Cawthra was not of the landed gentry class. He came from a class of Yorkshire weavers. He had enterprise and started a woollen mill by cleverly diverting the watercourse which outraged the locals of Guiseley in Yorkshire. This necessitated his having to invent a kind of steam engine instead for his mill which eventually broke down. He ran into debt, just like D'Arcy Boulton, and he immigrated to the United States. He kept himself in funds there by making and peddling peppermints in upstate New York. Perhaps the locals did not take to him as "Brit" so he came north and slowly headed for York. On the way up with his peppermint business he made commercial contracts. Trading was in his Yorkshire blood. He was a loser and not young.

I have to quote from his first 1806 advertisement for an apothecary shop in York which for variety of items carried outdid any drugstore today: -- suits, dresses, hats, knives, and forks, scissors, silver watches, maps, pictures, bedding, tobacco, brandy, lime juice, and lastly 20,000 Whitechapel needles. His store prospered, his daughter married a merchant, his injured son Henry obtained the use of a Crown grant of land in Toronto Township. By 1812 Joseph Cawthra had established extensive commercial contacts in New York and Montreal so that when the war came he profited greatly as a supplier. His sons John and Jonathan, under Lieutenant Robinson served in the 3rd York militia in 1812 and 1813 at Queenston and Detroit. Cawthra's store was one of the few not looted in York in 1813. By 1820 J.S. Baldwin wrote Quetton St. George that "Cawthra has more money by him than any man in York".

In 1818 for £500 currency Joseph Cawthra bought a house at the northwest corner of Front and Frederick Streets from the Baldwin Family. Some historians claim that Mackenzie operated his Colonial Advocate from this house and that it was from here in 1822 that his presses were thrown into the lake.

If this is so, which I doubt, Mackenzie must have been a tenant. Joseph's son, John started a successful business in Newmarket; Jonathan Cawthra simply disappeared; and young William stayed with papa and learned "frugality and capacity in business". Their aim was to make money and hoard it in mortgages and property. Neither the Boultons, nor the Robinsons, nor the Hagermans, nor the Hewards, nor the Ridouts, nor the Baldwins asked Mary (Turnpenny) Cawthra to tea.

The Cawthras were fit to be tied by the inhibitions to carrying on business, and became Reformers. In Upper Canada there was a value called "currency" reckoned in pounds, shillings and pence. This currency was set as worth ten percent more than British pounds, shillings, and pence, but there was no coinage for it at all. Specie was almost non-existent. What coins there were were British pounds, United States dollars and old Spanish dollars that were often cut into bits. Two of these bits made a quarter dollar. Many of the coins were defaced and had to be weighed to determine their value. Merchants issued paper, much in the way Canadian Tire Stores do today, as well as copper tokens. The Bank of Upper Canada issued copper tokens for pennies and halfpennies. Besides this array there were in circulation notes of hand, and IOUs issued by the well-to-do. Some of these might have to be discounted. Much service was paid for in firewood. All this was not the fault of the Family Compact but any merchant who did not favour Reform would have been crazy. The Cawthras were Reformers and supported Mackenzie.

Lieutenant-Governor Sir Peregrine Maitland regarded all Reformers as incompetent and uninformed, and were epitomised by the "reptile", Mackenzie, who was disturbing the house of assembly. He said of Joseph Cawthra that he was "a shoemaker for many years who now keeps shop -- he can barely write". Joseph's son, John, in Newmarket ran as a Reform candidate in Simcoe County in the election of 1828, and had the effrontery to defeat William Robinson, John Beverley's brother. Voting lasted a week, and the voter had to show his land patent (often recently acquired, as are Liberal party memberships for provincial seats in Toronto), stand on a platform and declare his vote publicly. My records show that Cawthra won by one vote, 71 to 70. In the following election of 1830 John Cawthra lost to Robinson and never tried again. In 1834 old Joseph Cawthra became an alderman of the new city of Toronto in the Reform sweep that made Mackenzie mayor, but he served only the one term. William Robinson did run again successfully.

In 1837 Sir Francis Bond Head said, "if you dispute with me you will only quarrel with your bread and butter". This was taken up by the "contras" who began drilling at Newmarket and who took to firing at buttered loaves of bread on a fence. John Cawthra regarded this action as practicing for an armed rebellion and made his way down to see William. For all he knew, the rebels were after Cawthra family deposits in the Bank of Upper Canada. Wars might be all right, but rebellions were bad for business. So the Cawthras sat tight and sold supplies to the militiamen.

Mackenzie, of course, escaped. A calvary unit led by a Boulton, and an infantry unit led by another Boulton, both from Cobourg, were upstaged by the men of Gore and Allan MacNab. All through 1838 alien "contras" from across the border made forays. A foray came to Cobourg in 1838 and was captured. A Boulton was on the bench, another was Crown Counsel, and such was the spirit of co-operation that a young Boulton very decently offered to defend the ruffians. He got them off lightly even though one absolute cad had tried to poison his dog.

I can not conclude this discourse at the year 1837, nor with the arrival of Lord Durham, nor yet again with the arrival of Lord Sydenham at Toronto in 1841. What happened to the mutually supportive aristocratic Boultons? What happened to the cautiously pro-reform not quite upper crust Cawthras? What happened to Mackenzie, and what does it reveal about the emergence of aristocracy in Ontario?

Joseph Cawthra outlived D'Arcy Boulton and lived till 1847, leaving about $800,000. D'Arcy died poor. William Lyon Mackenzie was permitted to return to Upper Canada in 1849 and defeated George Brown in a provincial election in 1851. When Prime Minister Sir Allan MacNab (who had sought so hard to catch and kill Mackenzie in 1837) needed a ferret to look into the muddled finances of the United Canadians under democracy, who should he pick to do it but a member of the legislative assembly, William Lyon Mackenzie. Mackenzie thereupon discovered that the Methodist archangel Egerton Ryerson, our glorious minister of education, had taken hold of the total funding for education for both Canadas and for safekeeping had put it into his own bank account and was drawing interest on it himself.

But what about an aristocracy? Did one arise? William Cawthra, who was landed as a baby from a boat at York in 1803 and whose mother had never been asked to tea at the Grange, died in 1880 leaving an estate of over three million dollars -- a sum in our money today possibly worth fifty million dollars. He had no children and all his relatives (who had done all right when well-to-do grandfather Joseph had died in 1849) looked forward. But there was no will. All Cawthras agreed, but not the Mulocks and Crowthers, that lawyer James Crowther had burned the will. For years those millions were the root of evil. The family attempted to ascertain for sure that William's brother, Jonathan, was dead and had died without issue.

The Cawthras of the second generation were called by John Ross Robertson "the Astors of Upper Canada" and they girt themselves with the glory of social supremacy and wealth. Did they stand for election? No. Did they go into professional practices? No. Did they write useful books to help immigrants? No. Did they run for city council? Of course not. Did they initiate manufacturing or commercial enterprise? Why bother. Did they get a coat of arms? Yes. Did they buy Rolls Royces? Yes. Did their ladies get presented to court? Yes. Did they travel? Indeed yes. But, did all of this make them part of the new aristocracy? Two Cawthras literally went mad from self-esteem trying to prove it.

At this point, an account of what might be called the last skirmish of the rebellion offers an appropriate concluding commentary on the emergence of an Upper Canadian Aristocracy. In the 1840s William Cawthra was still living at the bottom of Frederick Street. Just north of him on the corner of King and Frederick Streets was an oyster bar kept by a gentleman of colour named Blaxham. This oyster bar was patronized by the younger brothers of some of the spirited young gentlemen who threw Mackenzie's press into the lake. Today such an establishment would be called a singles bar. William Cawthra was kept awake by comings and goings of young gentlemen and ladies in cabs at night to and from the oyster bar, especially by those entering and later emerging from a couple of rooms Blaxham had above the singles bar in case anyone should get tired of being single.

Mr. Blaxham was a tenant. The owner of the property was the mayor of Toronto, who, as it happened, was a Boulton. William Cawthra thereupon charged the mayor with living off the avails of prostitution. The mayor being an absolute gentleman stood down from his seat in council and there was a preliminary hearing to decide what sort of things went on in Blaxham's oyster bar. The girls said they came for oysters, all but one who said she came to see a young Mr. Hagerman and he did not seem to need oysters at all. Consequently, a charge was laid by the Crown against Mr. Blaxham for keeping a house of ill repute. Mayor Boulton gave evidence at the trial that he had no idea of what was happening in the building, and to be on the safe side he also said that the building was in his father's estate and was not perhaps legally his entirely even if he had known. The patrons came for the fun and Hagerman brought some nuts to throw at the girls. After the mayor gave his evidence the Justice said "Your honour, as chief magistrate of the city of Toronto, would you care to join me on the bench?" Mayor Boulton went and sat with Mr. Justice John Beverley Robinson and together frowned on poor Mr. Blaxham who was fined and lost his oyster licence.

The Reform papers expressed outrage. Tory papers ignored the case. Methodist papers alluded to the likelihood of God's wrath descending on the Hagermans. William Cawthra had stirred the political pot, improved the tone of property values on Frederick Street, and it had cost him nothing. I don't really know who won.

Orangemen and the Rebellion of 1837

Cecil Houston

THE SASH

Chorus

It is old and it is beautiful
And the colours they are fine
It was worn at Derry,
Aughrim, Enniskillen and the Boyne.
My father wore it when a youth
In bygone days of yore
And it's on the Twelfth I love to wear
The sash my father wore.

Verses

Here I am a loyal Orangeman
Just come across the sea.
For singing and for dancing
I'm sure that I'll please thee.
I'll sing and dance with any man
As I did in the days of yore
And on the Twelfth I'll proudly wear
The sash my father wore.

Now you look after me, old boy
And I'll look after you.
And we'll keep the old flag flying,
The old red, white and blue.
Our cry was, No Surrender,
No republic we will join.
And it will always be as now
Derry, Aughrim and the Boyne.

Oh, it's now I'm going to leave you
Good luck to you, I'll say
And when I'm on the ocean
I hope for me you'll pray.
I'm going to my native land
To a place they call Dromore
Where on the Twelfth, I'll proudly wear
The sash my father wore.

(Traditional song of Orangemen around the world)

MACKENZIE'S PETITION TO PAYNE

To Payne in a dungeon, as he sat on his throne,
  Some traitors in Canada prepared a petition;
That he for his friends would Republican own,
  And prefer them his favorite sons of sedition.
                         For this way their aim
                         Wherever they came.
To set all in confusion---the world in a flame,
  And they begged he'd instruct them how best to convey
Peace, freedom, and comfort from Canada away.

"My sons," says Tom Payne, "You are welcome and well,
  'Tis a jubilee here when the world's in trouble;
Each demon rejoices when subjects rebel,
  But when a kingdom's o'erturned our triumph is double,
                         Our dungeon doth ring,
                         Cui Malo we'll sing;
My sons, dip you hands in the blood of your King'
  Join the 'CENTRAL COMMITTEE,' and quickly convey
Peace, freedom, and comfort from Canada away."

"Great Sir," they replied, "we approve of your plan,
  Each virtue we'll banish, each truth we'll disown;
With the 'States,' in their fury, we'll join heart and hand,
  Hurl COLBORNE from York, and WILLIAM dethrone.
                         Their backs we shall ply
                         In a transport of joy,

But Great Britain arose, with old Ireland to stand,
  And said, to repulse them, Canadians will join;
Whilst William defends fair Albion's dear land,
  The conquest in Canada, SIR JOHN, shall be thine:
                         Then let them draw near,
                         It soon shall appear
That Britons are ever still strangers to fear;
  We'll soon trim those Radicals who strive to convey
Peace, freedom, and comfort from Canada away.

                         -OGLE R. GOWAN

(Taken from William Shannon's collection, The Dominion Orange
Harmonist, published in Toronto by MacLear and Company in
1876)

108

ORANGE YEOMANRY OF '98

I am an humble Orangeman --
  My father he was one;
The mantle which the sire once wore
  Has fallen to the son;
He ranked with those who quelled their foes --
  The foes of Church and State;
The gallant Orange Yeomanry
  Who fought in 'Ninety-eight!

The light which led their spirits on,
  O'er battle-field did shine,
Each breast was Freedom's temple pure,
  Each heart was Freedom's shrine;
As sinks the day in glorious ray,
  Some sunk -- and bright their fate --
The gallant Orange Yeomanry
  Who fought in 'Ninety-eight!

Behold the Orange peasant, or
  The Orange artizan;
Go view his home, observe his ways;
  You'll find it is his plan,
Thro' woe or weal, with godly zeal,
  True men to imitate --
The gallant Orange Yeomanry
  Who fought in 'Ninety-eight!

To guard the Faith which Luther preached --
  The rights which William won,
The Orangeman relies upon
  His Bible and his gun;
He prays for peace, yet war will face,
  Should rebels congregate;
Like the brave Orange Yeomanry
  Who fought in 'Ninety-eight!

"Who fears to speak of 'Ninety-eight?"
  This was the silly note
Of one who was afraid to put
  His name to what he wrote;
He was afraid -- they're all afraid --
  They know we'd gag their prate,
As did the Orange Yeomanry
  Who fought in 'Ninety-eight!

In peace, like watchful silent stars
  Can Orangemen remain;
In war, their energies are like
  The surges of the main;
And each true-hearted Orangeman
  Would smile, though death await,

As did the Orange Yeomanry
  Who fought in 'Ninety-eight!

(Taken from <u>The Sentinel Orange and Patriotic Song Book</u>)

Militia and Regulars

Mary Beacock Fryer

There were two distinct phases to the rebellion era. One was the two internal risings of December 1837, first on Yonge Street north of Toronto, and second in the London District. At the time the 24th Regiment, which was the Upper Canada garrison of British regular troops, had been dispatched to Lower Canada. Volunteers drawn from the sedentary militia of Upper Canada came forward in numbers sufficient to cope with the two risings.

The second phase was much more serious. Canadian rebels who had sought safety in the United States and their American supporters staged a series of raids that terrorised communities near the border. In response to these disturbances, what amounted to nine regiments of British regular troops were moved into Upper Canada. The professionals were kept inland, because of the frequency of desertions if they were stationed at border posts. By order of Sir John Colborne, commander of forces in both the Canadas, the regulars were held in readiness to counter-attack when a border incident occurred. Front line troops at border posts were incorporated militia regiments. Militia were not likely to desert to the United States, whereas the republic was a promised land for many British troops.

The most serious of the border disturbances were at Pelee Island in late February and early March 1838, and at Windmill Point near Prescott that November. The last incident was the damage to the Brock Monument at Queenston Heights in April 1840. Then in September 1841 some "republicans" planned to blow up the locks of the Welland canal, but they were foiled.

The following British troops served in Upper Canada during the rebellion era (not all were there at the same time):

Full Name	Headquarters
1st (King's) Dragoon Guards (one squadron, 89 all told)	Niagara-on-the Lake
1st (Royal) Reg't of Foot	London
24th (Warwickshire, in 1838 2nd Warwickshire) Reg't of Foot	Toronto, Drummondville (Niagara Falls)

32nd (Cornwall) Reg't of Foot	London
34th (Cumberland) Reg't of Foot	Amherstburg
43rd (Monmouthshire Light Infantry) Reg't of Foot	Drummondville
65th (2nd Yorkshire North Riding) Reg't of Foot (3 companies)	Kingston
71st (Highland Light Infantry) Reg't of Foot *Mackenzie tartan trews!	Montreal, one company to Brockville
73rd Reg't of Foot	Brantford
83rd Reg't of Foot	Kingston
85th (Bucks Volunteers) (King's Light Infantry) Reg't of Foot	St. Thomas
93rd (Highland) Reg't of Foot	Toronto Drummondville
Royal Engineers (officer corps)	Toronto, Kingston
Royal Sappers and Miners (about 30 served)	Toronto, Kingston
Royal Artillery (328 officers and men)	Toronto
Royal Marines (about 30 served)	Kingston

Blacks and the Rebellion of 1837
Melody Brown

INTRODUCTION

John Graves Simcoe, this country's first Lieutenant Governor, dreamt of an Upper Canada that would be just like the England he loved. In 1793 Simcoe introduced Canada's first Anti-Slavery legislation; eventually in 1834, slavery was abolished in all British Colonies including British North America. After Simcoe returned to England in 1798 his dreams were shattered, as once again, free Blacks were in danger of becoming slaves if the United States gained control. Peter Russell who took Simcoe's seat was in favour of the institution of slavery and he "tried to bring back the right to import slaves".[1] Black settlers feared for their freedom; therefore they were willing to defend their new home even if they did not receive government support.

Support was eventually given but it did not come easily because:

1   it was hard to find white officers willing to command Black troops

2   poor Black men with families did not want to enlist for six months as required by the force

"Blacks had a proud tradition of war service by the time the Rebellion of 1837 occurred. The War of 1812 saw the formation of segregated militia units, called 'Coloured Corps", under command of white officers. Both freemen and slaves fought for the British and were rewarded land and freedom for their distinguished service".[2] Blacks again, as we know, went to war in the Rebellion of 1837, prepared to protect their freedom and new found rights in Upper Canada.

In November of 1837 the first official Black companies were formed. It was not long after their formation that their strength became evident, as a result a call went out encouraging more Blacks to volunteer.

CONTRIBUTIONS MADE BY BLACKS

When Mackenzie's Rebellion broke out, Blacks in every community were more than happy to enroll in the forces. Their first opportunity came December 11th, 1837 when the General of Militia wrote to Thomas Runchey of Niagara asking him to form a corps of Blacks and by December 15th James Sears had 50 willing colored men under his command.

On the night of December 29, 1837 these Negroes were on duty along the bank of the Niagara opposite Navy Island when the rebel ship 'Caroline" set sail for the "adventurous enterprise". The Caroline was carrying supplies and men to Navy Island, with the intention to give the rebels support for an all out attack on Upper Canada. However, Commander Drew caught up with the Caroline and set it on fire.

Josiah Henson , a Minister and founder of the all Black Dawn Settlement in Dresden, Ontario, commanded a company of Black volunteers. They were part of the Essex County Militia. Josiah Hensen's Unit made a great contribution to the rebellion, as it was recorded: "When the Schooner 'Anne" manned by the rebels and their sympathizers, sailed down the Detroit river firing it's gun into the town of Sandwich it's fire was immediately returned. The captain eventually lost control of the Anne which drifted ashore on Elliotts point Henson's detachment with other units took possession of the vessel. The ship's crew was made prisoner and the vessel and contents became a prize of war".[3] Henson's unit helped to defend Fort Malden from Christmas 1837 to May 1838.

Another company of Blacks was Captain Caldwell's coloured corps. The corps consisted of 123 Blacks. During the rebellion they were stationed at Fort Malden for two months. Benjamin Turner, a Black who settled in Oro TOwnship about 1830, was given the honour of serving as a Private in Captain Edward Lally's Company -- the 1st Simcoe Militia.

On December 18, 1837, 18 of Hamilton's Blacks signed a loyal statement of people of colour, professing that it was their duty as loyal men to give their support to the government of the Queen during the present crisis. This led to the formation of a company under Captain William Allen, Lieutenant Leonard Mead and Sergeant John Tory.

The Hamilton Gazette later reported: "On Tuesday about 100 of the 5th core Militia arrived here, on the same day from 150 to 200 additional volunteers left town to join Col. McNab on the Frontier. Among these were almost every coloured man in town".

COMMENDATION TO BLACKS

Blacks gave their all to defeat Mackenzie's Rebels. They did their best because the prize they were fighting for was worth much more to them than anything the war could ever produce -- their freedom.

Blacks were commended for their service during the Rebellion. These were some of the comments made about their loyalty and good service. M. Jarvis wrote, "this is to certify that the colored company commanded by Captain Allen did their duty while on the frontier, in every respect of my satisfaction...should they be employed again they would not disgrace Her Majesty's service".[5] Allan McNabb wrote: "the men under my command were always ready and willing and they conducted themselves to my entire satisfaction".[6]

On March 6, 1838, the Lieutenant Governor, Sir Francis Bond Head, acknowledged the loyalty of Black Canadians, and reported the following to the legislature of Upper Canada: "When our coloured population were informed that American citizens sympathizing with their suffering had taken violent possession of Navy Island for the double object of liberating them from the domination of British rule and imparting them the blessing of republican institutions, based upon principle that all men were born equal, Blacks hastened in wagon loads to the Niagara Frontier to beg from me (Sir Francis Bond Head) permission ... that they might be allowed to be foremost to defend the glorious institution of Great Britain".[7]

END OF THE REBELLION

By the spring of 1839 the threat of the rebellion had passed and slowly colored units were disbanded. In spite of the good service provided by the Blacks, in the eyes of many they were still looked upon as former slaves. A good example of such an attitude can be found in the Chatham Journal after the coloured company of Chatham was disbanded. "They all left apparently in high spirits, with music and colors flying, cutting up the greatest "nigger shines" imaginable, and followed, if not by many good wishes of our inhabitants, at least with one that they may never return again".[8]

Some units were kept in service after the Rebellion, to work on road construction, or as a local police force during construction of the Welland Canal".[9] In 1842 Captain Cameron's company was Chatam's main fire fighting force and during this time their swift action prevented a major fire from spreading in Chatham.

CONCLUSION

Today, Blacks in Canada can be proud of their forefathers. They were fighting not only to hold on to their freedom but to ensure that those who followed them would live in a country where they would not be in bondage. In spite of the lack of support, they knew that they had to defend their freedom and they did so courageously.

NOTES

1   Hill G. Daniel, _The Freedom Seekers, Blacks in Early Canada_, 1981 p. 17.

2   OBHS, _A Proud Past A Promising Future_, Teachers Guide, 1986 p. 14.

3   Hill G. Daniel, _The Freedom Seekers, Blacks in Early Canada_, 1981 p. 118.

4   Ibid., p 121.

5   Ibid.

6   Ibid.

7   Ibid.

8   Op. cit., p.123

9   The Ontario Black History Society, _A Proud Past A Promising Future_, Video & Teachers Guide, 1986, p. 14

Joining The
Rebellion

David Gibson's Involvement in the Rebellion in Upper Canada

Douglas Fyfe

In Sir Francis Bond Head's account of the rebellion in Upper Canada, William Lyon Mackenzie overshadowed those who joined him in revolt.[1] By stressing that Mackenzie was responsible for leading the rebellion, Bond Head hoped to draw attention away from the claims made by the rebels as a group. And yet William Lyon Mackenzie did not lead alone, nor had he won the support of other Reformers solely through his personality. Men such as David Gibson had been drawn to rebel against the government because of their world view and their own perceptions of what Upper Canada was and what it should become. They were not the blind followers which Bond Head portrayed, risking their lives for a dream conjured up by Mackenzie's treasonous fancy.

David Gibson was born in 1804 in Scotland, north of Dundee, in the parish of Glammis.[2] His family, like many in the area, lived from farming and weaving. According to the Parliamentary Report from the Select Committee on Handloom Weavers, Scottish weavers were:

> ...intensely theological, often religious, well-versed in all the intricacies of Calvinism, severest critics of the ministers' discourses and keenest of heresy hunters, scenting it from afar in phrase or simile, therein only being strong conservatives...[3]

T.C. Smout has added to this picture of David Gibson's contemporaries that "they were notorious radicals in politics... though some people thought them too fond of argument to take effective action to gain their ends."[4]

As weaving went into decline at the close of the eighteenth century, the status of most weavers fell below that of even casual labourers. From their earlier critiques of politics emerged a stronger voice based upon essential rights and elementary notions of human fellowship. They also became enthusiastic supporters of such causes as Owenite communities, the universal general strike, the Chartist land plan and the United Scotsmen.[5]

One of the Gibson family's responses to the poor prospects in their area was to apprentice fifteen-year-old David for five years to be a land surveyor.[6] His father, knowing that David was to be away from the family for long periods, implored him to read the Bible, follow the Sabbath and "conduct yourself so that you may be respected and loved by all that have occasion to deal with fearing God."[7]

In the other letters from David's father a fierce independence and sense of duty are also evident. Although these attitudes were present in the son, they co-existed with a romanticism which his father did not express. Sir Walter Scott had written Waverly in 1814 when David was ten and like Scott, David enjoyed fishing in Scotland's streams and shooting.[8] He also made excursions to areas imbued with the romantic. He recorded in his diary that "At Kinnell Church saw the large spur that Ogilvy of Beauchamp carried off from the Field of Battle"[9] and "went to the craigs of Loch Brandy (where) we saw the house on the top of the hill in which Lord Airly stayed after the rebellion when in a state of madness."[10]

In 1825, David Gibson came to Upper Canada at the age of twenty-one. He was eager to see his new home as being a land of plenty divided fairly among all inhabitants. In a letter to a friend he stated one of his first impressions; "as to the management of government affairs, there is very little room for complaint, the House of Assembly men are put in by their farmers, or freeholders and everything is done agreeably to the desire of the generality of the people".[11] However, his view quickly changed. His surveying drew him into areas isolated from the capital where he was able to observe that there were many problems that needed to be addressed.

David Gibson soon became politically active. The first temperance societies for York and York county were founded in 1831. David Gibson was the latter's first President,[12] a position which no doubt drew him into conflict with the way some members of the Family Compact used control over liquor licenses to maintain power.

In 1834, David Gibson ran successfully for the House of Assembly, with the support of Mackenzie, as member for the 1st Riding of York county.[13] The petitions Gibson presented in the House were mostly concerned with roads and land grants.[14] He also introduced several petitions calling for the government to pay for the expenses incurred by friends of Mackenzie in protesting his expulsions from the House in 1833.[15]

David Gibson made few speeches in the House of Assembly. One of the topics he did speak on at length, though, was the establishment of land reserves set aside for the Anglican church in the colony.[16] As an indirect warning to the Family

Compact of possible consequences of their plans, he alluded to the elderly woman who threw her three-legged stool at the English Bishop who had come to preach in Edinburgh on the command of James VI. Her action had popularly been seen to have begun the wars of imposition of English worship in Scotland in the seventeenth century. According to David Gibson's argument, plans to support the church of the minority not only went against the wishes of the majority, they also went against the Bible; "The command given to the Apostles when they were sent forth to preach the gospel, was not get one-seventh of the land where you preach." David Gibson believed that the giving of money to a church by the state led to laziness on its part. Money should be earned; no church in Upper Canada should have the support of the government.

Overall, though, in 1834 and 1835 David Gibson appears to have been content to support the policies of Mackenzie and have his influence felt on such committees as the Committee on Grievances.[17] Outside the House of Assembly, he exerted influence as a director of the People's Bank[18] and as a director of the York Agricultural Society.[19] Another one of his functions was as the chairman of the Constitutional Society.[20] This group was devoted to demonstrating that the government in the colony was behaving unconstitutionally by disallowing a large proportion of the Bills of the House of Assembly. According to the Society's argument, the combination of such action with the lieutenant-governor's reliance upon a non-elected Executive Council ignored the elective principles becoming established in Britain.

By the end of 1835, the radical Reformers had escalated their attacks. David Gibson joined six other members in attempting to halt the allocation of funds to all the functionaries of the Executive branch of the government.[21] This tactic had its precedent in the English House of Commons in the seventeenth century and had been attempted in Lower Canada only a few months earlier. It was one of the last devices available to the radical Reformers to effect change from within the government. As in Lower Canada, it failed to change the practice of the government in the colony.

In July of 1837, the resolutions of a committee of Reformers were read.[22] The committee consisted mostly of Scots and the Calvinist notion of government responsibility was prominent. David Gibson was the first person listed after the Chairman and the Secretary. The committee stated in part that:

> Government is founded on the authority and is instituted for the benefit of a people; when therefore, any government long and systematically ceases to answer the great ends of its foundation, the people have a natural right given them by their Creator to seek after and establish such

institutions as will yield the greatest quantity of happiness to the greatest number.

Similar words had informed the American Revolution and had provided legitimacy to demonstrations throughout England and the Canadas.

In August of 1837, a meeting of the electors of York County was held on David Gibson's property. Resolutions were passed classifying themselves as 'radical Reformers', renewing their pledge of allegiance to the Reformers in Lower Canada and reiterating demands for an accountable executive power in the Province.[23] David Gibson also chaired a similar meeting in Vaughan[24] which members of the Orange Order attempted to disrupt. One week previously, Mackenzie had been set upon by supporters of the Order, but in Vaughan the Reformers had prepared themselves with each man having a solid oak or hickory stick. The Orange 'Ruffians':

> ...expostulated about the clubs and Mr. Gibson frankly told them that their unmanly conduct on the Friday was properly resented by the farmers, and that hereafter at public meetings they (the farmers) would teach them and such as them the peace...

The 'desperadoes' "sneaked off without beat of drum."

David Gibson also attended meetings in Markham[25], Lloydtown[26] and Toronto[27] in the months prior to the rebellion. In September and in November several hundred men met on his property for what had been publicized as turkey shoots. In his diary he referred to them as trainings.[28]

Despite David Gibson's eventual acceptance of radical politics, he was not as radical in 1837 as William Lyon Mackenzie. Gibson appears to have viewed the trainings on his property as demonstrations of unrest to government. Such demonstrations were the next stage in a logical sequence of escalating demands for change. News of the plan to march on the government in December was withheld from him until several days before the march itself. Even on the night before the march, he may have been calling for the gathering of men to be used merely to indicate the degree of unrest in the colony. Nevertheless, he noted in his diary on December the fifth that he "came to Montgomery's Inn in Arms against the government with 150 or 200 others about 6 A.M.".[29]

Despite having acceded to the wishes of the other rebel leaders, he still attempted to exert a moderating influence. After the burning of Dr. Horne's home by Mackenzie, Gibson and Samuel Lount prevented the burning of Sherriff Jarvis' house in Rosedale.[30] Gibson also provided protection for the government supporters that had been captured by the rebels. After the first shots were fired upon the rebel base at

Montgomery's, David Gibson tried to lead the prisoners to safety. He was pursued and shot upon by Judge Jones. Nevertheless, as James FitzGibbon related, "Mr. Gibson prevented his men from firing at Mr. Jones, saying that they were beaten, and he entreated them that no more blood should be shed ... After this Mr. Gibson permitted his prisoners to depart unhurt."[31]

David Gibson then fled to Rochester, New York. He was firmly committed to the rebellion by this time and joined Mackenzie in seeking followers throughout New York state.[32] He continued to avoid being involved in the fighting though. In 1838, when a raid commenced upon Kingston, he remained in Rochester to keep the rebel's accounts.[33] Gibson and Mackenzie had a falling out shortly thereafter due to Mackenzie's criticism of Dr. Rolph and a disagreement over money.[34]

Although distance was maintained from Mackenzie after 1839, David Gibson never expressed shame for the part he played in the aborted rebellion. In September of 1838 he had written to Dr. Rolph "I consider it had come to the pitch that we must submit to the distaste of an unprincipled Governor as a parcel of slaves or resist. The latter of which I consider was most honourable whatever might be the result."[35] His language was just as strong in 1840 when he wrote to his half-brother summarizing the life he had tried to lead since he had last seen him in Scotland, "I have seen considerable of the World, and acquired considerable property and have in endeavouring to sustain my rights endangered considerable property, but I have no doubt but the final result will be to my credit for all I have done, I am a full believer in the principle of 'do no wrong and suffer no wrong'".[36]

The rebellion had many immediate consequences for the Gibsons. Not only was their home burnt down and a £500 reward offered for the capture of David Gibson, but also many neighbours and relatives were arrested. Mrs. Gibson and the children moved into the home of the Cummer family several lots north of their old home.[37] In that undoubtedly crowded house, they lived through the months of late Winter without hearing more than rumour as to where David was. When word did come, the family again uprooted itself and moved to the United States to develop a new life, Mrs. Gibson returning only occasionally to collect rent from the old property.[38]

In letters written in the 1840s, David emphasized that he was not involved with the rebels after the arrival of Lord Durham.[39] The British government's having sent an individual with the will to change the government of the colony apparently satisfied one of his primary aims. Instead, a position was found for David as an engineer on the Erie canal, a new farm was bought and another son was born, George Washington Gibson. In these years he appears to have been happy to hear of politics in the Canadas without being politically involved anywhere.

David Gibson was pardoned in 1843 and returned to a politically transformed York County in 1848. After an unsuccessful attempt to represent his old riding in the House of Assembly, he accepted a prominent position from the Commissioner of Crown Lands, Dr. Rolph.

Was David Gibson a radical Reformer? Yes, in relation to many of the other Reformers. However, he was conservative in his attempts to deal with the difficulties in the colony according to established precedents -- something which he referred to as his duty to follow. He also tried to discourage Mackenzie's attempts to diverge from those tactics which were founded on British traditions and instead to follow republican models. His life not only provides an interesting illustration of what leads an individual to join a rebellion, but also emphasizes the diversity of the Reform leadership.

Notes

1. Sir Francis Bond Head's Narrative, cited in Kingston Chronicle and Gazette, (April 13, 1839).

2. Letter from James Lyon Minister, (March 26, 1825).(Unless otherwise noted, all letters referred to are from the David Gibson collection).

3. T.C. Smout, A History of the Scottish People 1560-1830, (London, 1985, Fontana Press), p. 395.

4. Ibid.

5. Ibid. p. 395 and E.P. Thompson, The Making of the English Working Class, (London, 1961, Penguin Books), p. 326.

6. Letter to David Gibson from his father; July 1819, Letter to David Gibson from his uncle; March 11, 1821.

7. Letter to David Gibson from his father; July 1819.

8. David Gibson's Diary; May 17 & 24, 1823; July 12, 1824.

9. Diary; November 23, 1823.

10. Diary; July 11, 1824.

11. Letter from David Gibson; April 27, 1827 in Patricia Hart, Pioneering in North York, pp. 8-15.

12. Christian Guardian, March 19, 1831.

13. <u>Toronto Patriot and Farmer's Monitor</u>, October 18, 1834; Colanial Advocate, March 13, 1834; Diary; October 6, 1834.

14. <u>Minutes of House of Assembly</u>, 1835.

15. <u>Ibid</u>., February 18, 1835: Petition of John Hugill and 75 others; and February 28, 1835: Petition of William Reid Senior and 53 others.

16. <u>Kingston Chronicle and Gazette</u>, December 24, 1836; and February 25, 1837.

17. <u>Minutes of the House of Assembly</u>, January 23; February 17; and March 16, 1835; <u>Christian Guardian</u>, March 18, 1835.

18. Diary, November 1, 1835.

19. George Walton, <u>The City of Toronto and the Home District Commercial Directory and Register with Almanack and Calendar for 1837</u>, reprinted by the Toronto Branch of the Geneological Society, September 1987.

20. <u>Colonial Advocate</u>, February 13, 1834; and the Catalogue to "Rebellion in the Canadas 1837-8, An Exhibition presented by the National Archives of Canada", Robert J. Burns <u>et al</u> curators, Ottawa, published by National Archives of Canada, 1987, p. 11.

21. <u>Minutes of the House of Assembly</u>, April 13, 1835.

22. Charles Lindsey, <u>The Life and Times of William Lyon Mackenzie</u>, Vol. 2, (Coles fascimile of the 1862 edition); (Toronto; 1971 Appendix D, Coles Publishing Company).

23. Toronto <u>Constitution</u>, August 23, 1837.

24. <u>Ibid</u>.

25. Diary, June 18, 1836 and September 19, 1837.

26. Diary, August 5, 1837.

27. <u>op</u>. <u>cit</u>. Colin Read and Ron Stagg, pp. 50-53.

28. Diary, October 30, November 11. Another "training" may also have been held on the Sheppard farm, see <u>Toronto Patriot</u>, November 3, 1837. According to notes made by Gibson for an anonomous pamphlet denouncing Mackenzie's post-rebellion activities "Gibson asked Mr. Bidwell if the trainings were illegal he said no my object was to keep within the requirements of the law"., Gibson papers pp 22-24.

29. Diary, December 5, 1837.

30. <u>Patriot</u>, June 23, 1843 and letter from David Gibson to Dr. Rolph, pp. 21-7.

31. <u>Patriot</u>, June 23, 1843.

32. Elsie Graham Sumner, "Activities of the Canadian Patriots in the Rochester District", in <u>Ontario History</u>, 1944, vol. xxxvi, pp. 29-30.

33. <u>Ibid</u>., p. 31.

34. Letter from David Gibson to John Rolph undated (21-7). In another letter, Gibson's anger at Mackenzie is transparent. In this letter he refers to a pamphlet by Mackenzie as being "pregnant with the characteristics of its author -- fulsome egotism, erratic, irrelevant digressions, unscrupulous untruths, and nauseous repetitions of his alleged wrongs issued in the chaotic state in which they have coursed thru' his brain. There are in it a sufficiency of inconsistencies & contradictory statements to destroy its' general credibility in the minds of reflecting men. McKenzie (sic) gives me a (kick?) in passing and an invitation to enter the lists with him. But I feel very indifferent to his personal reflection which is falsely put, and disinclined to take up his gauntlet prematurely or till such time as I can do so with effect.", April 1854, pp. 24-7.

35. Letter from David Gibson to Dr. Rolph, January 6, 1852.

36. Letter from John Rolph to David Gibson, in Ontario Archives, John Rolph papers Reference (7-546 MS 533, Series A10, Letter 1843) A transcription is in The Gibson House Collection.

37. Letter from David Gibson, April 6, 1838.

38. Letter from David Gibson to his father, September 13, 1840.

39. Letter from David Gibson to his father, September 13, 1840.

The Commander in Chief from Huron

E. Jayne Cardno

"In appearance he was a tall, fine, soldierly looking man,but age gave him a stoop. His features were good, with a large nose, and he always wore a close cap, even under his hat. He was never seen without this cap, and the legend is that his ears had been cut off. He spoke English fairly well, and was considered eccentric. He was the first agricultural settler, and there is an interesting story of how the first sheaf of wheat grown in Huron was cut by Madame Van Egmond in the Year 1829 or 1830."

Robina and Kathleen Lizars provide a rare picture of Colonel Anthony Van Egmond in their work In The Days of The Canada Company published in 1896.

He was born in Holland in 1778. Evidence suggests he was a direct descendent of Count Lamoral Von Egmont, a knight of the Golden Fleece, who figured prominently in the political affairs of the Netherlands, but who ultimately was executed.

Two and a half centuries later Count Anthonius Jacobus Wilhelmus Gisbert Lamoral Van Egmont, known in Canada as Colonel Anthony Van Egmond would die before being tried for treason. He had led a magnificent European military career defending his native Holland. His untimely death in the Don Jail, a result of his political beliefs and struggles in his newly adopted country, likely prevented his execution.

In Holland in 1794 Van Egmond was a soldier in the Dutch army when Napoleon invaded. He was conscripted into the French forces. For the next eight years we find no trace of his activities. We do know that in 1802 and 1803 Van Egmond was in Mainz, Germany serving as an official in the courts. Sometime around 1808 he married Maria Susanna Elizabeth Deitz of Mainz, Germany. Their first son Constance was born the same year.

Reports by Van Egmond's contemporaries, William Lyon Mackenzie and Sir John Colborne insist that he was a veteran campaigner, fighting both for the British and under Napoleon. At Waterloo he met Sir John Colborne who was to become Lieutenant-Governor of Upper Canada from 1828 through to 1836. The Lizar sisters in 1896 wrote "His military career on the continent covered a period of 25 years, ... during which he received 14 greater wounds and many lesser, all in the front."

Van Egmond immigrated to Pennsylvania in 1819. He and his family remained there for eight years before following the trail of the Black Walnut in 1827. With a large migration of Pennsylvania Dutch he settled in Waterloo County where he rented a farm until he found what he wanted.

It was not long afterwards that he met John Galt, superintendent of the Canada Company. Van Egmond became interested in this project of opening and settling a million acres of land known as the Huron Tract, and he was appointed an honourary agent. His major task in this position was the construction of the Huron Road from Wilmot to Goderich (number 8 highway). Van Egmond also facilitated the hiring of 3 innkeepers to establish hostels at 20 mile intervals along the road. He became the fourth, establishing his tavern, Ross, just west of present day Seaforth.

Ironically, it would be concerns with the Canada Company, particularly its officials and unfulfilled promises, which would be the strong motivation behind Van Egmond's actions in 1837. In 1835 meetings were held by the Huron Union Society for the purpose of protecting members from wrong and injustice. Anthony Van Egmond was elected president. In September 1835 it was resolved that all hope for change had vanished: people should prevent settlers from coming to the Tract by publishing their woes. Colonel Van Egmond was requested to publicize the misdeeds of the Canada Company.

In 1836 Colonel Anthony Van Egmond was the Reform candidate for the District of Huron. He was defeated by Captain Robert Dunlop, brother of the popular Tiger Dunlop who was well supported by well-to-do English and Scottish families in the more populated Colborne area. Perhaps people associated Van Egmond with Napoleon as suggested by Professor Kerr, an excellent authority on Van Egmond. Certainly, he being from Europe and not one of the majority Anglo Saxon settlers with close allegiance to the crown made him more suspicious when denouncing practices of governing authorities.

Professor Kerr also notes Van Egmond's flamboyant writings suggesting that his style involved much exaggeration. This was a style that did not enhance his credibility or assist his cause. The following quote reflects well Van Egmond's feelings. He charged that Thomas Mercer Jones had deliberately surrounded himself by:

"old aristocrats and young idlers: half-beggared would-be-gentlemen, half pays and no pays, cashiered officers, mushroom aristocrats, etc, etc, creatures either half worn out or but half made knowing nothing and capable of nothing; and with more than ten pounds of pride for every penny in cash at their command ... The Canada Company's viceroy here soon found out that, if appointed to some office, they would swell his court and prove fit tools for they most intended mischief; but if not, hunger would make them bark and yelp, and by it he himself be hindered in getting and keeping all things here himself in his own way; and get them soon pledged; magistrates, commissioners of the court of requests, coroners, registrars, clerks, etc., etc. This done, his court was swelled indeed -- all gathered around him were as flies do around a lump of sugar. Eight or ten of them would usually form his horseguard on his journeys through the Tract, make Chesterfield bows to him and act quite equal with the courtiers of olden times -- when insulted, nay kicked, merely reply "thank you Sir"."

Mackenzie and rebellion were the last resort for Van Egmond. More than once the Colonel was quoted as telling the settlers: "If you want anything you're going to have to fight for it." In sheer anguish he wrote in 1837:

Having found but very few men in the Province, with hearts in their bosoms, I would advise all and every male in Upper Canada to dress in petticoats and betake themselves to the spinning wheel.

Van Egmond had exhausted all avenues of peaceful reform when his thoughts turned to force, and he succumbed to the ideas of William Lyon Mackenzie. In 1837 he wrote:

Ancient as well as modern histories, and in fact experiences made by ourselves, teach us, that our present disease requires the strongest of remedies, and we, the patients, a radical cure and no palliatives, humbugs. Although an ex-soldier of thirty years schooling and practice myself, I have always considered the pacificator, reconciliator, a nobler man than the greatest military hero, and have proved this by my past writings in favour of reconciliation, until 1836, when I felt convinced in my mind, that it was of no use anymore.

Van Egmond was in Toronto late in November 1837. Here, he made contact with Mackenzie and his followers. Having set the date for attack Van Egmond returned to his Huron home and immediately had to return to York for the December 7th action. Why such quick, arduous journeys were made we are not certain.

The colonel arrived early on the seventh of December but found only a few hundred men of whom some 200 were properly armed. He vetoed Mackenzie's plans for immediate attack on the city. Mackenzie in a rage threatened to shoot the old colonel. A compromise was reached and a diversion planned.

Van Egmond has left us a confusing trail of papers which provide our only knowledge of his thoughts and participation in the rebellion. Two documents "His Plea to The Honourable Commissioners of the Court of Enquiry" and his statement made on being captured, seem obviously intended to help extricate Van Egmond from his terrible plight. Professor W. B. Kerr in 1940 analyzed these documents carefully. He states "while most details are true others are construed to provide innocence". The gist of these statements is the claim by Van Egmond that he was kidnapped by Mackenzie's rebels and forced to give military direction. It was a useless effort as the officials had much better information and only served to discredit him.

From prison he wrote his "Pleas to the Commissioners of the Court of Enquiry." In it he described himself:

> ... as a man rapidly advancing to the age of seventy years, with the use of but one arm, one leg and one eye any more, and by a consumption of eighteen months since reduced to nearly a mere skeleton, and now quite innocently incarcerated in this city jail, without even a rag of my own to rest on or lay on at night time, and until this morning without any other bodily nourishment but prison bread, and the little that was given to me by other prisoners.

Van Egmond died January 5th, 1838 of pneumonia in the prison hospital. His son Edward, whom had been pressed into the local militia under instructions from William Dunlop was part of the unit which ransacked his father's Inn taking all his personal papers. Thirteen thousand acres owned by the Colonel were confiscated by the colonial government. There is no record of any compensation.

Van Egmond remains an obscure, misunderstood figure. While the county of Huron readily venerates such figures as Galt and Dunlop, there are few that have even heard of Van Egmond. Those who have, repeat his name softly, hesitantly, some with contempt. What was his role? What did he do for Huron? He died in prison, untried for treason.

Local historian James Scott wrote in 1966 "it is curious that an event as remote as the 1837 uprising ... should set the tone for remote Huron's thinking and its attitude to all things military ... The reason was Col. Anthony Van Egmond". One must still agree today.

Joseph Gould:
The Reluctant Rebel

Allan McGillivray

Although Joseph Gould, an entrepreneur, industrialist, parliamentarian, Quaker and rebel, died just over 100 years ago, his name is still prominent in Uxbridge. Visitors to the local Friends Burial Ground note that his monument is the largest one, contrasting with the simple stones of his friends and neighbours. His name is on the meeting house historical plaque, and the Uxbridge plaque in town. Joseph Gould Senior Public School was built about fifteen years ago. The Joseph Gould Mechanic's Institute and Library marked its centennial this year. His portrait hangs at the Uxbridge-Scott Museum which is located on former Gould property near where he was born. Museum visitors ask about him and wonder how a Quaker became involved in a rebellion. Here is a brief outline of his story, and how he worked to improve the lives of the backwoods settlers in Upper Canada.

The Golds were Irish Quakers who settled first at Germantown, near Philadelphia. They later moved northwestward in Pennsylvania to Catawissa on the east branch of the Susquehannah River. From there, two brothers came north to Upper Canada with the Timothy Rogers settlers. William Gold settled immediately in Uxbridge Township about 1805. Jonathan Gold spent about three years near Yonge Street before acquiring a property close to his brother. There a son named Joseph was born to Jonathan and his wife on December 29, 1808.

Joseph soon showed that he had a rebellious nature. He attended the Ezekial James log school which was near the farm. There he studied from the old Webster speller. One day, he noticed on a page that "gold was the name of a metal and Gould was a man's name". He went home and announced that from then on he was going to have a man's name, and eventually the entire family took on the name Gould.

At eighteen years of age, Joseph apprenticed with Jared Irwin on Yonge Street to learn the carpenter trade. He also picked up some sawmill experience which became valuable later. Back at Quaker Hill in Uxbridge, he began erecting houses and barns.

In the spring of 1830, something happened that led to a turning point in his life. A growth developed in his nose. The search for a cure took him to see Dr. Widmer in Toronto. There he had to stay several weeks while the treatment was applied. What was there to do for a twenty-one year old from the woods in the growing capital of the province? That was no problem for Joseph. He was already interested in politics, so he talked to both the Tory and Reform members of the legislative assembly. He watched the legislature in action and read all the newspapers. By the time Joseph arrived back in Uxbridge Township, he had decided that he did not like the aims of the Tory Family Compact.

The following spring he spent some time in Pickering where he gained more sawmill experience, and from there he went to do some building at home. He then decided to leave to go to Ohio where he had cousins, and he packed his tool chest. However, one Sunday on the way back from the Meeting House, his neighbour, Ezekial James, told him that carpenters were needed at Uxbridge. Joseph consequently unpacked his tools.

In 1832 he rented the Clergy Reserve lot north of the James farm so he could plant some wheat. He cleared some of the land, and it was said that he could clear more in one day than most other fellows. Joseph needed a place to put the wheat after harvest so he decided to build a barn. John P. Plank had acquired Lot 29 in the 6th Concession, and had started to build a dam and sawmill where Elgin Pond is located. Joseph approached him about cutting some lumber, but Mr. Plank said the mill was in disrepair, and he could not be bothered working at it. He offered to sell Joseph the 200 acres with a log house, barn and the mill site for $1,200 with no interest and five years to pay. After some difficulty, Joseph got the mill running, and began his first business venture in the Uxbridge valley at 24 years of age. A post office was opened in Uxbridge in 1835. Up to then, the hamlet had been called Uxbridge Mills. Joseph Gould did not select this name. It was named after the township, an act which followed the tradition of naming the first post offices after the townships in which they were located.

Joseph subscribed to William Lyon Mackenzie's newspaper. He read it from cover to cover, digesting Mackenzie's grievances against the government, and then went into the hamlet to tell his friends and neighbours. This led to him being called upon to speak at public meetings. Joseph Gould worked so hard to get Mackenzie elected each election that he was chosen to lead the canvass for votes in Uxbridge and the surrounding townships. He became upset at Mackenzie's setbacks and expulsions, and began signing petitions against the government as early as 1831. He was working to have the Clergy and Crown reserves dismantled, and to have a form of local self-government set up. He also opposed the Orange Lodge, and was greatly bothered by the fact that his father, because he was formerly a citizen of the United States, could not vote because of the Alien Act.

During one of the elections, Joseph was attacked by four overly zealous Tories. He said he knocked the first one down and the others fled. However, a warrant was issued for his arrest. When three constables came for him, he jumped on a fast horse and got away. He rode to Pickering where Squire Leys helped him to get off with just a nominal fine.

Joseph's life was not all wrapped up in sawmills, carpentry and politics. He liked to go to balls, dances and wild parties. He said he "gallivanted first with one girl and then another".

He was proud of the fact that great store was set by his word. This reputation he guarded very carefully throughout his life.

As the political situation in the province came to a head in 1837, Joseph found himself having second thoughts about it. He felt that the grievances were going to be looked after, and that there was no need for violence. This was probably his Quaker upbringing coming to the fore. He was reluctant to get involved with the events that were unfolding.

A week before the actual rebellion took place, Mackenzie held the last of his secret meetings at Stouffville. There, Joseph told Mackenzie personally that they should not go ahead for things would get better. For his pains he was called a coward.

The day before the planned attack, Joseph found himself with forty or fifty men from Uxbridge, Scott, and Brock. They wanted him as leader, but he said he refused to get involved in violence. They reminded him about his many speeches against the government, and wondered if he had become too cowardly to follow through. At that point, he reluctantly joined them.

Joseph Gould's account of what took place during the next few days has survived. That evening, his group arrived at Montgomery's Hotel on Yonge Street. He said Mackenzie was going through mail bags and holding up letters. There was neither order nor discipline. Joseph was afraid they would be caught off their guard, so he posted pickets for the night.

The next morning, Captain Matthews was sent with a group including Joseph's older brother, Joel, to fake an attack by the Don bridge. The main force was to attack from the north. Before this could be achieved, word arrived that the troops were coming. Among their weapons, the soldiers had two small field pieces. Joseph said one was in the hand of a friend. It fired grape shot over their heads, and broke from the hemlock trees dead branches which rained down on them. The other was fired low and dangerously, and he did not like it. A ball hit a sand bank, and put sand in his face. Captain Wideman was killed nearby, and Fred Shell from Brock was shot through the shoulder.

Joseph found himself with a small group on the west side of Yonge Street. They were unable to get back to Uxbridge, and set up camp. On December 13, their campfire gave them away, and they were captured. As most other makeshift prisons in Toronto were already filled with prisoners, Joseph and his friends were housed for several weeks in the Legislative Council Chambers. (Joseph later was fond of recounting that that was the first time he took his seat in Parliament.) Among his fellow prisoners was John Plank of Uxbridge.

At his trial, Joseph was asked to state his situation. He said he owned a small farm and sawmill at Uxbridge. The questioners then requested "What more do you want?" He replied, "I want my political rights", and started into the list. They cut him off, and he was sentenced to be locked up in Fort Henry at Kingston. He remained there until he was released in October of 1838 upon promising to keep good behaviour for three years.

The Uxbridge-Scott Museum is in possession of an attache case which Joseph sent in 1838 as a gift to his neighbour, John Plank, of Uxbridge. In a letter to Mr. Plank, Joseph said he could not figure why they kept him locked up when some of those who had talked him into becoming involved were free. Joseph also asked Mr. Plank to keep the fences on his farm in repair so the cows would not damage his apple trees.

Joseph returned to Uxbridge following his release and soon had his sawmill running again. In January of 1839, he married Mary James, daughter of his old neighbour, Ezekial James. Maybe that is what Ezekial had in mind when he tried to discourage Joseph from going to Ohio.

When Joseph Gould first arrived at Uxbridge in 1832 to buy John Plank's sawmill, Uxbridge Mills already consisted of a tavern, a store, a gristmill, and blacksmith and cooper shops. However, following the Rebellion, for about the next fifty years, Uxbridge centred around the enterprises of Joseph Gould.

In the 1840s he built grist and woollen mills. He represented Uxbridge under the Township Commissioners' Act. From 1842 to 1854 he was Home District Councillor. He was elected Provisional Warden of Ontario County in 1852, and was the first reeve of Uxbridge township. He was elected the first member for the new riding of Ontario North in 1854. He was re-elected in 1857-58. His opponent was his old enemy,

Ogle R. Gowan, head of the Orange Lodge in Ontario. Joseph Gould was never defeated in any election in which he ran.

In 1847 he registered a plan for lots along Mill Street on his property. This area became known as Gouldville. In the early 1850s he bought the Hamilton property surrounding the west side of Uxbridge containing 280 acres, for $19,000. Within two years, he sold the mill site, just east of the library, for $11,000, and in one day sold lots amounting to $10,000. That gave him $2,000 profit, and he still had 250 acres left.

In the 1850s Joseph built a grammar school at his own expense, and was on the school board for many years. He built the Mansion House Hotel after the railway arrived, and in his will left a relief fund to provide money for families of men who had become poor spending money at his hotel. He had been on the Mechanic's Institute board since its start in 1859, and initiated plans to build the Joseph Gould Mechanic's Institute in 1886, but died before it was erected. He left directions for its completion, and it was opened late in 1887, 100 years ago.

Joseph and Mary Gould had eleven children. The sons followed his lead, and were involved locally in milling, merchandising, banking, and politics.

Joseph died on June 29, 1886.

The following is a short poem which he included in his letter from Fort Henry to John Plank in Uxbridge:

"Life is but a day at most,
Sprung from night in darkness lost;
We poor mortals here but borrow
A moment's joy from months of sorrow."

Switzer of Streetsville and Mackenzie

Bruce Peel

I - POLITICS IN TORONTO TOWNSHIP

Martin Switzer of Streetsville appears only as a small footnote in two reminiscences of Upper Canada in the 1830s; but his friendship with, and support of William Lyon Mackenzie, and his part in the 1837 rebellion in the Western District, warrant him a more significant place in the history of the times. Like other settlers he experienced the hardships of pioneering in the bush in Toronto Township, and like many another disgruntled farmer he was an ardent Reformer. When the rebellion broke out he fled from possible involvement, but a sanguine forecast of a rebel victory heard in an inn, caused him to deviate from his course. In Yarmouth Township his enthusiasm helped to recruit rebels to march to join Dr. Charles Duncombe's army at Scotland. Because Martin's treason was committed far from home, and because of his successful avoidance of arrest for eight months and his family's prompt removal afterwards to Illinois, the Switzer story is largely untold.

Martin Switzer was born in 1778 in County Tipperary[1], Ireland. In late June, 1804, he sailed with his wife and baby from Dublin on the brig _Atlantic_ bound for Boston. During four years in northern Massachusetts (later the State of Maine) the new immigrant experienced democracy in the form of the New England town meeting; no wonder that later in Toronto Township he would be frustrated by the lack of local government, and by the bureaucratic control exercised by the Family Compact in York.

In 1808 the Switzers moved to Elizabethtown, New Jersey, where Martin followed his trade of blacksmithing. The family might have remained there permanently had it not been for the War of 1812 and the strong anti-British sentiment which lingered afterwards. In 1819 the Switzers were associated with a group of Irish Protestant families who, under the sponsorship of James Buchanan, the British consul in New York, were granted land northwest of "muddy York". On January 9, 1820, Martin set off with part of his family to carve a farm out of the forest three miles north of the future town of Streetsville.

During the early years Martin, like all his neighbours, was principally engaged in the back-breaking work of cutting down the forest, removing the stumps, and burning the felled trees. The only glimpse into the domestic life of the family is found in the 1827-28 accounts ledger of William Proudfoot, the general merchant.[2] The Switzers sold two barrels of ashes and received a credit of £6-2s-3p. On one occasion their purchases included twelve yards of linen for a daughter's wedding trousseau, and bombazine to trim the women's hats. The head of the household, when he visited Proudfoot's, indulged himself in the purchase of a shilling-worth or two of snuff. When Switzer became active in support of Mackenzie in Toronto Township he had passed his fiftieth year.   In appearance, as recorded years earlier on the manifest of the Atlantic, he was of fair complexion and stood five feet ten inches. After years of swinging a pioneer's axe and wielding a smith's hammer he was well-muscled and noted for his strength; on one occasion this saved Mackenzie from being roughed up by the local Orangemen. More significant to the story of political events in the 1830s was Switzer's personality. Inclined to be impetuous, he was a man of strong political opinions, and he was forthright and fearless in expressing them.

A collection of pioneer reminiscences has preserved a description of Martin's confrontation with officialdom in York, where he travelled to pay his taxes:[3]

> When Martin Switzer of Churchville went to Toronto (York) to pay his taxes to Treasurer Powell of the Home District, he entered complaint against these conditions. He figured up the tax paid in his own township and said that he could not see what the people were getting in return, since they were left without bridges even, save such as they built themselves.
>
> "I think," said Switzer, "some of this money must be misappropriated in Toronto."
>
> "Look here, my man," Powell insolently responded, "Your business is to pay taxes. It is for the gentlemen here in Toronto to say how they shall be spent, and if I hear any more seditious language from you I shall have you put in York jail."

Grant Powell, the man Martin challenged, was the personification of the York establishment, the Family Compact. Son of the former chief justice, he was clerk of the powerful

Legislative Council and holder of several other offices as well. Mackenzie would complain, with justification, that Powell could not give proper attention to his manifold duties.

The Toronto farmer did not remain silent about the incident:

> Switzer spread the story on his return home, and anger, savage enough before, was fanned into a white heat. It is no wonder that people rose in arms. They would have been less than men if they had tamely submitted to the insolence and incompetence of office to which they were daily subjected.

Twice in 1831 Switzer appeared before the Court of the General Quarter Session, each time as a witness on behalf of a person charged with assault and battery. What was this sober farmer of mature years doing involved in brawls? Their cause and nature went unrecorded, but they may have been rooted in politics. When a new monarch ascended the throne -- on this occasion William IV -- it is customary for groups of subjects to send felicitous addresses wishing him a long and prosperous reign. In the summer of 1831 Mackenzie toured the province urging that such addresses include a listing of the political grievances of King William's loyal subjects in the colony of Upper Canada. At the same time Tory leaders suggested that people express their happiness with the status quo; at least one such address originated in Toronto Township.

Over the Christmas season that year Switzer gathered signatures to petition the government for money for road improvements in the northern part of Toronto Township. That December, Mackenzie the gadfly of the Assembly, had been expelled from the House, and accused of printing defamatory statements in the Colonial Advocate. At a by-election on January 2, 1832, he was re-elected. Two days later, back in the House, he tabled eight road improvement petitions, No. 5 being that of Switzer and fifty-three other settlers.

The politician on March 21, 1835 once again tabled a road improvement petition headed by Switzer. Unfortunately this attempt by Martin failed because at the end of that session, as in the 1832 session, the Legislative Council vetoed all bills coming up from the lower House for approval. Had Upper Canada had municipal government under which taxes could be levied for local improvements and the work overseen by local men, might the 1837 rebellion have been avoided? Certainly Lord Sydenham gave this reform high priority in 1841.

In the 1830s politics were rough and boisterous, as Mackenzie would experience on three occasions in the Streetsville district. An Act of the Upper Canada parliament had redrawn the constituency boundaries making Peel County the Second Riding of the Home District, with Streetsville its sole polling centre. Mackenzie chose to stand for election in this new riding. On a cold January evening in 1834 the local Reformers organized a banquet in Mackenzie's honour.

Along the border between Toronto and Trafalgar Townships lived a group of hard-drinking, hard-fighting Irishmen known locally as the Town Line Blazers. Their leader, Henry Cole, was an avowed enemy of the Reform movement and of Martin Switzer.

The night of the banquet the Reformers gathered at Mother Hyde's hostelry,[4] some having come from as far away as the Scotch block (a Mackenzie and Reform stronghold). The men took their places in the dining room and Malcolm McKinnon was asked to say the blessing Gaelic. The solemn hush was suddenly and rudely broken:

> With a bang the front door was forced open and Harry Cole, followed by an immense crowd of Town Line Blazers, burst into the room ... The Reformers were overcome and chased out into the cold with empty stomachs, whereupon the Blazers sat down and did full justice to the feast. All the time Mother Hyde, undaunted, ceased not to rail at the invaders. This caper soon passed into local folklore.

In the provincial election of October, 1834, Mackenzie won handily with 334 votes to his opponent's 178. During the week-long polling Mackenzie was a guest in the Switzer home. This display of friendship for the radical politician roused the antipathy of Martin's Tory and Orange neighbours, and marked the beginning of his tribulations. He later wrote, "Since that time those people have had a bad feeling toward me, and done me many private wrongs."[5]

In 1836 Sir Francis Bond Head, the new lieutenant-governor, called a provincial election. At issue for Tory voters was the maintenance of the British connection and the monarchical constitution; they viewed the Reformers as favouring American republicanism. In no riding was the election fought with more bitterness than in the one centring on Streetsville, where the Tories and their bully-boys, the Orangemen, were determined to prevent the re-election of Mackenzie by any means.

On June 27, the opening day of the poll, Martin Switzer played a brief but dramatic role:

> Streetsville was the polling place for the Second Riding of York; and violence was apprehended on the day of nomination. A procession of Orangemen, an organization with whom Mr. Mackenzie was on ill terms, took place; the "Boyne Waters," "Protestant Boys," and "Croppies Lie Down" being played by the

band. They afterwards drew up in line at a point where it was necessary for Mackenzie to pass. Several were provided with loaded fire-arms, on both sides. One Switzer, a man of enormous muscular power, led the way through the lines; and Mr. Mackenzie followed unharmed.[6]

Had Mackenzie been prevented from reaching the polling station, presumably, he could not have filed his nomination papers and his opponent would have been elected by acclamation. In any case, by the end of the election Mackenzie had lost at the poll.

The politician afterwards charged that irregularities had occurred during the election. A long siege of ill health unfortunately prevented Mackenzie from assembling evidence until the end of the year. In the December 21 issue of his newspaper The Constitution he named Reform supporters throughout the Second Riding and asked them to provide him with data to support his allegations; Switzer was one of the thirteen men listed for the western part of Toronto Township. When the assembly refused to consider Mackenzie's appeal he publicized his charges in his newspaper on January 11, 1837.

These accusations roused the ire of the Streetsville Tories. Mackenzie, living in the city of Toronto, was out of reach but his friend Switzer dwelt among them. The attack on the farmstead came late at night; no doubt the terrified family watched the destruction of property from the dark windows of their home, a brief account of which Switzer provided in the following newspaper notice.

Fifty Dollars Reward[7]

A band of ruffians, supposedly eight in number, names unknown, came to my Premises in Toronto Township, tore down one large Gate, carried it to the road and broke it up -- went and threw down the Orchard Fence -- came to the Workshop and broke the Windows -- pulled down the palling or fence in front of my Dwelling-House -- threw down the Gates of one of my Fields, and put it in the Creek. I will pay $50 reward on their apprehension and conviction; and I request the aid of every friend of peace and quietness to bring them to justice.

Martin Switzer

Toronto Township, Feb. 3, 1837

In a neighbourhood just emerging from the pioneer phase no doubt most gates were crude barriers -- a couple of poles across the gap -- but Martin had taken pride in fashioning proper gates, the iron fixtures crafted in his own smithy. The destruction of his gates smacked of spite.

In the summer of 1837 Mackenzie busied himself organizing local political unions through the province; the purpose, he claimed was to convince the government that the mass of people wanted reform. In August the "Churchville Affray" took place. Mackenzie attempted to hold a rally at Churchville, which was three miles from the Switzer farm. Six hundred men turned up. Several Orange lodges were in attendance. Suddenly a horn was blown, and fifty men armed with clubs rushed to the edge of the platform where the politician stood. An attempt was made to push him down among his enemies. At the same time two women drove a wagon into the crowd, and the Orangemen reached under the hay for the shillelaghs concealed there. In the donnybrook that followed, Mackenzie escaped, surrounded by a phalanx of Reformers.

Four months later Mackenzie's rebellion broke out on the northern edge of the city of Toronto. On December 7th and 8th Mackenzie again passed through Toronto Township, now a defeated rebel chief in full flight.

II - THE RIDE TO YARMOUTH

On Tuesday, December 5, Martin Switzer heard a rumour that Mackenzie and his rebels were assembling on Yonge Street above Toronto. Two days later, the morning of the battle at Montgomery's Tavern, Martin, at his wife's insistence, fled.

> Came home and staid at home untill thursday morning at four o'clock when persuaded by my wife to leave home for my personal safety knowing that there were many who called themselves loyalists would be glad of an opertunity to injure me. At which time I left home with an intention of going to the United States untill I could be home with more safety.[8]

Mary Switzer had reason to fear for her husband, considering the ill-will he had experienced as a friend of Mackenzie. Further, in times of civil strife a blacksmith in his shop might be suspected of forging pikes and running bullets for the rebels. Locally, at the first intelligence of insurrection the Town Line Blazers had ridden off to defend Toronto, but on their return they could well be capable of mayhem.

In mid-morning the man in flight stopped at the inn of Caleb Hopkins, a Reformer who had earlier sat in the Assembly:

> On my way I stopped at Hopkinses inn in Nelson to feed my horse when I saw Charles Durand for the first time in my life to know him. He told publickley that he was in the Mail stage when it was taken by McKinzie and his partie, and he also stated that it was his belief that the Rebel army consisted

of between four and five thousand and that Toronto was in their poss(ess)ion at that time.

Durand was a young lawyer who the previous morning had been on the westbound stage when it was held up by Mackenzie and two accomplices. The stage turned back, but Durand had continued on foot toward his home in Hamilton. Two days after the meeting in Hopkins' Inn he was arrested and charged with treason.

That morning at the inn the other traveller had to reconsider his options:

> I also learned that I could not pass over to the United States as the lines were gauarded (sic). I then altered my mind and thought I would pay a long promised visit to an old acquaintance in the Township of Yarmouth, namely Elias Moore member of the P(rovincial) P(arliament) with whom I had been acquainted for nearly thirty years.

To sojourn among pacifist Quakers in a settlement far from the epicentre of the uprising seemed an ideal refuge. But was Martin aware of the well-publicized belligerency the men of south Yarmouth had exhibited at political rallies in recent weeks? Did the potential there for gaining support for Mackenzie's rebellion occur to him? The Switzer narrative was penned months after the rebellion, while the author was a state prisoner charged with high treason; since it was intended for the perusal of his judges, his statements must be read with a degree of scepticism.

Switzer as he rode westward may have played a significant part in spreading news of the rebellion:

> I invariably told every one with whome I conversed what Durand had told in public.

Much later the Executive Council of Upper Canada in considering the case of Switzer the prisoner would observe:

> He seems to have been at much pains to spread the news of the insurrection to the westward, and the account which he gave of it in the London District according to his own acknowledgement caused the adherence of many to the cause of rebellion.[9]

Martin was the third herald of rebellion to ride into the village of Sparta, the social centre of the American Quaker settlement. Finlay Malcolm of Bayham came first, then Elias Snider of Norwich arrived Saturday evening, December 9. He addressed a small gathering of men, and the nucleus of an armed corps was formed with the intention of marching to join the rebel army of Charles Duncombe at Scotland. While Switzer may have arrived on Saturday evening, it is likely that he reached Sparta on the Sunday.

Martin described his arrival in the Quaker settlement:

> When I got to Elias Moores I found that he was not to be seen. When I made myself known to Mrs. Moore she told me whare I could find him. I went four miles further where I found Mr. Moore at an Inn.

The traveller met Moore in Sparta, but the sitting member of the Assembly was not alone:

> There was also a party of armed men there which on receiving that intelligance from me concluded they would go and join Duncombs party.

Martin's chronicle is silent on events in Sparta over the next forty-eight hours, Sunday through Tuesday, but many of the rebels in their later depositions to the authorities would imply that their involvement was due to Switzer's persuasiveness. What excitement his arrival must have generated! Here was a man newly come from the centre of the rebellion, and one who claimed friendship with the leader Mackenzie. A grand rally was held on the Monday evening with Switzer as the keynote speaker.

The message of the "man from Toronto" was that in all probability Mackenzie with his four or five thousand men was in possession of Toronto the capital. Now what was needed to ensure that Lieutenant-Governor Sir Francis Bond Head would capitulate to the demands of the Reformers was a general turnout to demonstrate popular support; political reform in Upper Canada might be attained without firing a shot. Switzer was emphatic that local men must march to show solidarity with Mackenzie's rebellion. Martin gave his word of honour that what he had told them was the truth:

> He told us if he deceived us to lay his head on a block and cut it off.[10]

On the morning of Tuesday, December 12, the Sparta rebel corps, some fifty strong, assembled in front of Hitchcock's Inn. The men had armed themselves with whatever weapons they owned or were able to borrow. Captain David Anderson, a tavern keeper, supplied the lead balls for the muskets, while Lieutenant Joshua Doan, the tanner, provided several pounds of powder. The community collected a war chest of $70 to support their expeditionary force in the field; the largest contribution came from Dr. Duncan Wilson who would later be implicated in the Short Hills raid. At noon the corps of Spartans moved off, most of their number on foot, but some riding in the two commissary wagons.

In his narrative Switzer attempted to portray himself as an observer rather than a participant in events in Sparta and on the march to Scotland:

> I found the state of the country was such that I could not stay in that part in safety. Perplexed and having no place I could stay in safety, I imprudintlee resolved to come in company with that partie of armed men. I came down some distance before them to the Otter Crick and stopped at Pawlings Inn. I told the Mistriss of the House there was a party of men to be there that night. I requested that she would keep me a bed as I expected the house to be full.

The Spartans reached Richmond after nightfall, and bedded down in the inn. At midnight two riders, John Moore and Harvey Bryant rode in from Sparta. They conferred with Switzer, conveying a warning that mounted militia from St. Thomas would soon be in pursuit.

Moore had a second reason for coming to Richmond -- to persuade Joseph, his delicate teenage son, to return home. After dark the youth had taken a horse from his father's stable and ridden off to join the Spartans. The son refused to turn back, but the father repossessed the horse. A family tragedy was in the making. Five months later the son lay dying, while the father was incarcerated in London Gaol under sentence to hand for treason. Joseph, in his delirium, called for his father that he might seek his forgiveness for riding to Richmond that night, and thus being the cause of his father's misfortune. The Quaker community offered as surety their property - valued at $100,000 --if the authorities would allow John to visit his dying son. The request was refused.[11]

By an early morning departure the Spartans narrowly avoided an attack from the right flank. At Port Burwell the previous evening the local militia had mobilised, and through the night had been marching up the corduroy road toward its junction with the Talbot Road. They reached this destination too late, for the Spartans had passed.

A short distance beyond, a horse-stealing incident occurred. Two footsore young men stole two horses, a bay and a gray. A farmer ran out of his house and shot at them, wounding one in the arm. Switzer was not amused at this act of brigandage:

> I also left ... in the morning with them (the armed corps) for three miles (beyond Paulding's Inn) I disapproved of their conduct. I then left them and went on my way home and nevr saw them since.

Later, some of the marchers would claim that though Switzer rode ahead he remained in sight until they reached the Eleven-Mile Woods just before Scotland.

Dr. Duncombe would have been encouraged when Switzer rode in with the news of rebel reinforcements following close behind. He must have welcomed the information that they carried some gun powder, a war material of which his men were in short supply. Did Switzer loiter to witness the arrival of the corps he had helped to recruit? Was he still in camp when the disastrous news broke?

> I rode on and came to a place called Scotland and was taken up and taken before Dr. Duncomb. On telling my name and that I was one of McKinzie's supporters at Elections after he inquired of me what the newes from Toronto was. I told him as I did all others that Durand told at Nelson. He then let me go. I did not stay there ten minutes.

The men from Sparta reached Dr. Duncombe's encampment at seven or eight o'clock in the evening, and bivouacked. An hour later the camp was thrown into turmoil when a messenger brought Duncombe his first intimation that Mackenzie had been defeated seven days earlier. He learned further that Colonel Allan MacNab was advancing from Hamilton, and had reached Brantford with a strong militia force and artillery. A retreat was ordered. One voice was raised in objection, that of Captain David Anderson from Yarmouth. The rebels reached Sodom in the small hours of the night, and there the "army" melted away in the remaining hours of darkness.

Who was responsible for the uprising in Yarmouth, and the subsequent suffering it brought to the participants and their families? Certainly Switzer applied the bellows to a small flame and caused a larger conflagration. One young rebel, Lewis Norton, opinionated and articulate, had no difficulty in placing the blame on "Old Switzer", stating, "I do not think no man would have started from Yarmouth if it had not been for him."[12]

III - THE TRIBULATIONS OF AN EX-REBEL

Switzer, a few nights after the debacle at Scotland, arrived back at his farm home near Streetsville to discover that the Tory vigilantes had preceded him. He "found my house torn to pieces, my property destroyed and part of my stock taken away."

The returning fugitive found Mary, his wife, in the home of a married daughter:

> My wife as before would not suffer me to stay at home. She was afraid that my life was in danger from

those persons who destroyd my property. I left home
again and in three weeks was only home once.

The man wanted for high treason in the Western District
remained in hiding about his farmstead, or those of relatives,
until mid-April. Inquisitive neigbours were informed that
Martin had left the district on December 7, and was still in
the United States.

On January 4, 1838, the Upper Canada Gazette carried a
notice of a "writ of attachment" freezing the property of the
"absconding or concealed debtor" until he should pay a debt
owing a Streetsville merchant. Martin was in good company in
the Gazette for directly below his was a similar notice
impounding the property of William Lyon Mackenzie.

On April 15, two days after the hanging of Samuel Lount
and John Matthews in Toronto Gaol, a frightened Switzer again
fled his home district. He later stated:

After the exicution of Lount and Matthews I made up
my mind to leave Canada for I then. saw but little
prospect of any better time for Canada.

On the Illinois frontier, forty miles west of Chicago,
Martin purchased a partially improved farm. He was gone from
Streetsville for two and a half months:

About the first of July I returned home to make
preparations to move my family. I got home under
cover of night and staid unseen by my enemies for
some time expecting Lord Durhams proclamation, but
that was like every other good promised by Canadian
Governors. About the middle of August I ventured
out about my house and sold my farm for a trifling
sum and only got half of that trifle. The rest
remains due.[13]

In surfacing, Switzer seemingly thought no one in his
home district was aware of his treasonable actions in Yarmouth
Township. But Colonel William Chisholm of Oakville knew of
the outstanding indictment, and made application to have him
arrested. Now a wave of animosity was let loose on the
family. A son from Illinois, who arrived to assist in the move
to the American frontier, was jailed for a time as a suspected
traitor. When Martin went to collect a debt the farmer set
his dogs on him, saying that he would not have his land
contaminated by such a villain, but would speak to him only on
the high road. The Switzer orchard was largely destroyed,
and:

A few nights before I was arrested there were several
shots fired into my house.

In writing to the Attorney-General, Christopher A. Hagerman, the local magistrate James Magrath acknowledged the danger that the "notorious rebel Switzer" might suffer local violence, but promised that "there should be no lynch law here". Even the Executive Council in considering the Switzer case was apologetic about the intensity of hostility Switzer had experienced.

> It is impossible to allay or suppress this feeling in all cases suddenly, though its presence is productive of much serious evil.

Was Martin Switzer the last rebel captured in the province? In the official list of 885 persons arrested in Upper Canada for insurrection or treason the absence of his name seems a curious oversight. Was he captured too late to be included in the roster forwarded to the British House of Commons?[14]

Few rebel prisoners now remained in Toronto Gaol, but among these were John Moore and Harvey Bryant, the men who had brought the news of pursuit to the Spartans at Richmond. They were detained under threat of transportation. Switzer may have had Bryant as a cellmate, for each dedicated a prisoner's box to Mrs. Jane Bryant, and both drafted their petitions for a pardon on the same day. Martin, on the box he carved, inscribed a militant verse, the sentiments of an unrepentant rebel; the Tories, the party in power, were the real traitors:

> May vengeance draw the sword of war
> And justice smile to see it done
> And smite the traitors for the death
> Of Matthews, Lount and Anderson.[15]

The prisoner took counsel on how he might prepare his defence on the charge of high treason.

> I sent for George Ridoubt (Ridout) to take advise how to proceed. He advised me to stand trial as did every one else.[16]

The previous year Ridout had successfully petitioned the Colonial Office to overturn his dismissal from three offices by Sir Francis Bond Head; in so doing Ridout caused the haughty Sir Francis to resign his gubernatorial office. Martin rejected Ridout's advice; too many Switzer actions during the week of rebellion could not stand close scrutiny in a court of law.

> Contrary to all advise I resolved to petition (for clemency) under the Act. I rote my own petition. It was a long one. I told Sir George (Arthur, the new lieutenant-governor) a good story.[17]

Switzer, at the end of his sanitized narrative of events during the rebellion, sought to rouse compassion in his judges by describing his family's current situation.

> I am now upwards to sixty years of age. My hart broken wife and one son, which is blind are depending upon my for a support and through a journey of upwards to six hundred miles and in a strange cuntrie with very little means.

Mary Switzer and her sons on September 14 set off from Streetsville for Illinois with three wagons containing the family's goods and chattels, and with their herd of dairy cattle. The cows were to be the source of future prosperity as the rapid growth of Chicago created an expanding market for dairy products.

Martin would never know his good fortune that his treason case had not been considered at an earlier time. By late August in Quebec, the Governor-General Lord Durham had become concerned at the severity of sentences being meted out to rebel prisoners in Upper Canada. Now in late September the Executive Council in Toronto was aware that Durham was prepared to monitor decisions taken in the upper province.

On September 27, 1838 the Executive Council examined the Switzer case, and made its recommendations to the lieutenant-governor:

> The Executive Council have much hesitation in advising Your Excellency in the above case, according even to the most favourable account of prisoner's conduct -- he appears to have been highly criminal ... (etc.)

> The Council however in pursuance of the humane policy of His Lordship the Governor General, are willing to advise Your Excellency to allow the pardon of the prisoner on his finding security to keep the peace and be of good behavior for three years.

The bail demanded was $4,000, a substantial sum to raise in a rural community, but two of Martin's friends came forward as guarantors. Mackenzie's _Gazette_ on October 5 reported that Martin was now in Illinois having "left the debilitating air of Canada for a purer".

On December 7, the first anniversary of the battle at Montgomery's Tavern, and of the day when both Switzer and Mackenzie fled the Toronto area, Switzer the exile penned a letter to his old friend. In the conclusion he expressed optimism about the political future of Canada.

We begun the Sport in Canada. We made a bad
beginning but I look for a good ending and that
before long.

Notes

1. For Switzer genealogy see B. Wesley Switzer, <u>Tipperary</u>
    <u>Switzers, Descendants of John Switzer, of the Townland of</u>
    <u>Newpark, County Tipperary, Ireland</u>, (Brantford, 1987), p.
    415. This difinitive work includes articles on Switzer
    immigration and settlement in the Streetsville area,
    written by Mary Switzer Manning. See also her <u>From</u>
    <u>Southern Ireland to Southern Ontario</u>, (Streetsville,
    1980).

2. William Proudfoot, General Merchant, Ledger, p. 225.
    Baldwin Room, Toronto Metropolitan Library.

3. William Loe Smith, <u>The Pioneers of Old Ontario</u>, (Toronto,
    1933 in Makers of Canada, new series), vol. 2, pp. 177-
    78.

4. Rob Roy (pseud.) "Old times on the dividing line between
    Peel and Halton, in <u>Streetsville Review and Port Credit</u>
    <u>Herald</u>, May 29, 1913.

5. "Switzer's narrative accompanying his plea for clemency
    on a charge of high treason" in Civil Secretary's
    correspondence, Upper Canada sundries, RG5 A1, vol. 204,
    pp. 113188-93. Public Archives of Canada. The narrative
    exists also in a draft version, with slight variations in
    the text; RG1 E3, vol. 84, pp. 206-12.

6. Charles Lindsey, <u>The Life and Times of William Lyon</u>
    <u>Mackenzie</u>, (Toronto, 1862; Coles facsimile edition, 1971)
    vol. 1, p. 378.

7. <u>The Constitution</u>, February 15, 1837.

8. Switzer, <u>op</u>. <u>cit</u>.

9. Upper Canada Executive Council, Minutes; September 27,
    1838, RG1 E1, vol. 56, State Book L, p. 133. Public
    Archives of Canada.

10. Lewis Norton, London District Magistrates records of the
    treason hearings, vol. 2, RG5 B36. Public Archives of
    Canada.

11. <u>Mackenzie's Gazette</u>, quoting the <u>Rochester Democrat</u>,
    Mackenzie-Lindsey clipping file, MU1845, Envelope 864.
    Archives of Ontario.

12. Norton, <u>op</u>. <u>cit</u>.

13. Switzer to Mackenzie; Letter dated December 7, 1838, Ms. 516, Mackenzie papers. Archives of Ontario.

14. Canada. Return of an Address to the Honourable House of Commons, dated 8 May 1838 for <u>Return of the names and quality of the several persons arrested in Upper Canada, and placed in confinement in prisons in Toronto, and other places in the Province, on a charge of insurrection or treason; the dates of their arrest and discharge; and, if tried, whether by court martial or civil courts with the result of such trials severally; also the number in prison at the time of the list despatch.</u> (Ordered to be printed 25 February 1839) Reprinted in <u>Canada</u>, vol. 12, pp. 205-224. Irish University Press series.

15. Dorothy Duncan, "Prisoners boxes". <u>The Canadian Collector</u>, April 1971, pp. 7-9, illustrated.

16. Switzer to Mackenzie, <u>op</u>. <u>cit</u>.

17. <u>Ibid</u>.

The End Of The Rebellion

The Aftermath of the Rebellion

J.M.S. Careless

I am here to wind things up; but not to sum them up, or to weigh the proceedings of this Conference in one neatly packaged assessment. I do not pretend to deliver a final judgment on the Upper Canada Rebellion of 1837 (to some degree the jury is still out), but rather only to examine events and responses in the rebellion's aftermath. "Aftermath" that word can have huge, vague meanings: all the happenings since the Fall of Man might be deemed the aftermath of apple-eating in Eden. Hence I have checked my dictionary and found the term defined as, 'consequences, especially disastrous ones', and 'a second mowing, or a second-growth crop'. Not a great answer perhaps; except that there surely were disastrous consequences to the 1837 rebellion, and there surely was a second-growth crop thereafter. Accordingly, that is how I will address my subject: to deal mainly with the fierce and dangerous results that followed the suppression of revolt within Upper Canada in December, 1837, yet go on to note the brighter second-growth that subsequently arose as shown by returning security, reviving Reform and generally improving conditions.

We begin, then, late in 1837, just after the defeat of Mackenzie's Yonge Street rebels and the dispersal of those with Duncombe in the west. The Upper Canadian community at that juncture seemed in a fairly desperate state, racked by bitter depression, angry alarms and rampant reaction. Not that a bloody reign of Tory terror took place. Aside from the execution of Lount and Matthews, not to come till April, 1838, few died in punishment for rebellion -- and I am including here old Colonel Van Egmond, who succumbed as others might to the chill winter miseries of imprisonment. It was, however, an open season for hunting rebels, for tossing presumed traitors into jail on merest suspicion, to be left there without habeas corpus for months untried, and often finally released without any trial still. Confusion, fright and incompetence, rabid partisanship and sheer vindictiveness all could be involved. Loyal upholders of the constituted government denounced Reformers for treason on all kinds of assumption or pretext. Militia officers sent out detachments to track down rebel threats that were not much more than shadows, then turned their captive suspects over to the ready and willing magistrates. A British regular officer even caustically suggested that, 'the best cure for agitation in the country was to hang half a score of Militia Officers'.[1]

The fact was that there was scant security now for persons who had made decided radical noises before the rebellion, whether or not those signified actual complicity in armed revolt. Indeed, the thoroughly moderate impeccably uppercrust Reformers, William and Robert Baldwin, had to walk most carefully themselves. And the prominent Toronto radical James Lesslie, a close associate of Mackenzie, though not involved in the Yonge Street rising nevertheless was thrown in jail without charge, warrant or examination. He was kept there for 13 days, hotly protesting (ultimately to the Colonial Office direct), only to be released, at last, still uncharged.[2] In short, one can well perceive a harsh abuse of law and order by the very Tory champions of law and order. It lasted on into 1838, although the mass of Upper Canadians gave widespread indications that they supported their provincial government and that, whatever feelings might remain for Reform objectives, few people wanted to achieve them by armed violence or revolution.

Yet there also was a good deal of indication that forces outside Upper Canada did look to bring on revolutionary change by violence; forces based across the border in the United States. In a real way these elements gave content to Tory rantings about 'treason', for they clearly purposed the invasion and seizure of Upper Canada, from foreign soil and with foreign armed support. That project might reasonably be called treason, even if those who backed it saw it as liberation, with the all-but-certain blessings of annexation to the American republic to follow. Accordingly, the long series of border incidents and raids that resulted truly represented an escalation of an internal revolt (two brief outbursts) into an external, if unofficial, war. That much bigger conflict saw many more killed or wounded, executed or transported; and its threats and ravages were such that, if they did not justify repressive government in Upper Canada, they certainly went a long way to explain it. They even helped to keep the governing regime quite widely popular in an embattled province caught up in an aftermath considerably more destructive than the rebellion of its own home-grown radicals had been.

After the internal risings, the radical leaders had of course largely fled to the United States, Mackenzie, Rolph, Duncombe and others. Numbers of their followers and sympathizers also sought American shelter, making their way across a highly porous border that was beyond effective policing on either side. Yet these Canadian refugees, exiles-- or 'patriots' as they preferred -- became increasingly outnumbered by American allies who at first joined the patriot cause, then took it over. In the border states of New York and Michigan particularly, the spirit of Jacksonian democracy ran high during the 1830s. Here older anti-British or anti-imperial sentiments combined with Jacksonian ideals of equalitarian freedom, and with desires to bring Canada out of the darkness of British oppression into the sunlight of American liberty. But idealism rapidly became entwined with something else: outright American expansionism.

This expressed the confident dreams of manifest destiny, that the whole continent was ordained to come under the Stars and Stripes. It also embodied hunger for frontier land, freely promised to hopeful patriots in fertile Canadian acres; or good old American entrepreneurialism, sighting fresh opportunities for profit and power. Beyond that, there was the lure of adventure, not to forget simple dishonest ruffianism and lust for loot. In general, while not at all counting out real idealists and believers, the American-derived patriots widely appear as a fevered, rather scruffy lot. Yet in any case, they loomed larger and larger in the patriot movement during 1838. By that autumn, their new Hunters' Lodges served essentially to keep it going, when Mackenzie had long last credence, and his original confreres had been mainly left out on the sidelines. Thus in one of the last and bloodiest of the border thrusts -- at Prescott in November -- the attackers were almost wholly American. Over all, the radicalism of Canadian exiles in the patriot cause was steadily displaced by the expansionism of their American associates. Rebellion thus led on to military assaults on Upper Canada not experienced since the War of 1812.[3]

The combat at Prescott and the Battle of Windsor in December 1838, effectively mark the closing of this chief and violent stage of the aftermath. Nonetheless, border worries, with troops on watch and the possibilities of full-scale Anglo-American conflict, ran forward into 1839; not really to be settled, ultimately, till the Webster-Ashburton Treaty of 1842 disposed of continuing sore issues. By 1842, however orders and security had fully returned along the Upper Canadian border. By then, as well, economic depression had yielded to a rising era of prosperity and renewed British immigration. And since the spring of 1839, when Lord Durham's celebrated Report was received in Upper Canada -- amazing both Tories and Reformers, for very different reasons -- Reform revival was jubilantly under way.[4] Consequently, I think we may consider the time of aftermath, in its 'disastrous' sense, as pretty well over by the end of 1838, and in the sense of 'second-growth' as clearly displaying that resurgence by mid-1839. But this time-span now deserves a closer look, to examine major happenings that illustrate our theme. And so I will turn to very notable instances of border conflict, before concluding with the dawn of better days.

The first warlike episode was certainly that of Navy Island, where radical fragments left from the Upper Canada risings rallied on the Niagara frontier and were joined by American recruits to make a stand. This affair of late December and early January, 1837-38, might possibly be called Mackenzie's Last Stand, except that, of course it was not. If no military hero, he was politically indomitable and would live to fight another day: back in politics once more, in a Reform-ruled Upper Canada of the early 1850s, where he was to prove as zealous, bold and cantankerous as ever.

At any rate, with regard to Navy Island, in 1838, Mackenzie from his arrival there on December 14, took characteristically and busily to the paper work of politics. He proclaimed his new provisional government for Upper Canada (including Nelson Gorham, Silas Fletcher and Jesse Lloyd, Canadian comrades who were with him in exile and Lount and Van Egmond who were not). Military command was to be left to a dissolute and incompetent American patriot 'general' Renssalaer Van Renssalaer, whose most impressive feature was his name. And as at most a few hundred would-be warriors gathered to the radicals on Navy Island, so loyal militia some 200 strong took station on the Canadian mainland opposite. Yet Sir Francis Bond Head forbade an attack on the weak and ill-prepared rebel forces on the island, hoping instead to get Governor Marcy of New York State to extradite Mackenzie-- marvelously ignoring the fact that Navy Island was actually Canadian soil, hence extradition scarcely applied. But then Head's obtuseness well matched Mackenzie's rashness. I sometimes think that a television script on their roles in the Rebellion might be entitled 'Blockhead meets Firebrand'.

Be that as it may, a still-growing militia power blockaded Navy Island, and British regulars were ordered back from Lower Canada. Head appointed the bellicose Alan MacNab to command the troops on the Niagara frontier; the no less combative Captain Andrew Drew, ex-Royal Navy, took charge of a schooner-and-boat naval brigade. Here again was a recipe for trouble. While a small, early thrust might have swiftly cleared Canada's Navy Island without involving the United States, the delay, build-up and blockage pinned American attention to the border. Then MacNab and Drew were inspired to the bird-brained foray of the night of December 29, to seize and cut out the American steamer _Caroline_ -- which served to supply the rebels -- when she was lying in her harbour at Grand Island, in United States territory! This plain attack on legitimate sovereignty roused national wrath among Americans, impelling those along the border to sanction raids of reprisal against Upper Canada. But worse, the circumstances, or the myths, surrounding the destruction of the _Caroline_ inflamed American feelings still more. Long afterward, the widely circulated prints of those shrewd surveyors to Yankee perceptions, Messrs. Currier and Ives, showed a fiery ship of horror descending near-vertically over Niagara Falls, while bodies plunged from her decks into the watery abyss. One at least can say that the gallant Captain Drew lost the propaganda war.[5]

The propaganda war, however, was also forwarded by Mackenzie, no novice in that field himself. The weight of evidence is that the captured Caroline did not go over the Falls in flames, or with passengers aboard, but being tied up out of service, was towed away and set afire to drift. She went aground not far down-river, burned and broke up there, where he debris could be seen for years to come. But that did not stop the myth-makers, Mackenzie in the lead. In his Caroline Almanack he wrote:

> We witnessed the dreadful scene from Navy Island. The thrilling cry ran around that there were living souls on board; and as the vessel, wrapt in vivid flame, which disclosed her doom as it shone brightly on the water, was hurrying down the resistless rapids to the tremendous Cataract ... numbers caught, in fancy, the wails of dying wretches, hopelessly perishing by the double horrors of a fate which nothing could avert; and watched with agonized attention the flaming mass, till it was hurried over the falls to be crushed in everlasting darkness in the unfathomed tomb of waters below.

Such a dramatic report really should have been true. In any case, Governor Marcy and the American press took up and amplified the story of the Caroline's trip down the falls. Head himself -- never failing -- gave it official credit by gladly retelling it to the Colonial Office. Moreover, along the American side of the border citizens flocked openly to enrol in patriot ventures, while state militia and officials frankly showed them favour. The federal government of the republic was not so inclined to move to downright war with Britain. Nevertheless, its enforcements of neutrality in the border states was lax, to say the least, given the furore in public opinion and among state politicians there. Though federal troops were despatched to the New York frontier under General Winfield Scott, a truly capable commander in the War of 1812, his efforts to maintain neutrality were hampered by inadequate backing.

Meanwhile, new recruits flowed into Navy Island, though old ones left disheartened; Van Rennsalear was either drunk or quarrelling with Mackenzie; nothing was being accomplished beyond futile exchanges of cannon shots with the Canadian forces opposite. The failure of the Navy Island stand to rally Upper Canada to freedom was clear when Mackenzie left for Buffalo on January 4. There he was charged with breaching the neutrality laws, but was freed when local supporters put up five thousand dollars security for his appearance in court. And on January 14 the erstwhile rebel chieftain announced that his role at Navy Island was finished; that he would launch a new weekly in the United States to promote 'freedom and prosperity vs. despotism and poverty', a more congenial task.[6] The same day the patriot cohorts withdrew from the island, leaving their empty quarters for MacNab to occupy. It effectually spelled a final end to the Yonge Street rising, and to Mackenzie's career as rebellion leader. More than that, it largely marked the shift to an Anerican take over of the patriot movement. American quantity had already outranged Canadian quality in that movement; but henceforth its various episodes would heavily belong to American expansionists under American captains, even though some Canadian radical leaders and followers might still be involved.

Accordingly, the succeeding border incidents in the aftermath require less specific attention, since their general pattern is one of foreign military intrusions resisted by militia and regular troops; the War of 1812 reactivated, rather than the less deadly turmoil of domestic political strife. The first example arose on the Detroit River, only days after Mackenzie had left Navy Island. Western patriots and filibusterers collecting at Detroit openly organized and equipped an Army of the North West, despite the efforts of General Hugh Brady (Winfield Scott's counterpart in Michigan) to prevent arms-gathering there. Under the Irish-American 'brigadier general', Edward Theller, an attempt was made to take British Fort Malden at Amherstburg, vacated by the regulars who had been sent to Lower Canada. At the head of the broader offensive, Theller, and a party in the schooner Anne bombarded Amherstburg on January 9 and sought Fort Malden's surrender. But militia units returned the fire, the Anne grounded (our border history might have been altered by better charts) and Canadians boarded her to capture Theller and about twenty others. That temporarily checked the threat to western Upper Canada.

The next patriot move came in the east, at Hickory Island in the upper St. Lawrence near Gananoque. After considerable top-level conspiring on into February which certainly involved Mackenzie, along with Lower Canadian rebel leaders the actual strike at this Canadian island was launched on February 22 by several hundred American adventurers under Van Renssalaer and Pirate Bill Johnston, one of a type termed 'border ruffian'. Van Renssalaer, drunk again, failed to redeem his stature, while Johnston failed to bring him promised reinforcements. Instead of marching on Kingston, their expedition quietly melted away. It was however, quite characteristic of ill-led marauding pushes into Upper Canada, and also further disheartened the remnants of Canadian radicalism, while hardening popular resistance in eastern reaches of the province.

Nonetheless, other raids were under way in the west once more, starting again on the Detroit River, when on February 24 a band of American filibusterers seized Fighting Island in Canadian waters just off Sandwich. True, this force had largely been raised through the vigorous Canadian radical agent, Donald McLeod, self-declared commander of the 'Patriot Army of Upper Canada, Western Division', while Dr. Charles Duncombe, Mackenzie's son James and Nelson Gorham, member of Mackenzie's provisional government, had each participated in collecting American arms for the expedition. But the actual occupation of the island by some 150 patriots was a swift fiasco. Canadian militia and British regulars (now back again at Fort Malden) cannonaded, then charged the patriots' position across the frozen river, driving them to retreat to the American shore -- where a large crowd watched, and children blithely collected stray cannon balls that slid along the ice. The Canadians, too, gleefully dragged off the patriots' small cannon, an antique commandeered from a Michigan village common, christening it the 'Rebel Pup'.[7]

Generally speaking the border clashes so far had not been all that hard-fought. A grimmer episode began two days later, February 26, at Pelee Island, where another body of the 'western' invaders, about 400 strong, arrived by sleigh across Lake Erie. They were indeed Americans; only one former British subject proved to have joined in the raid. When the news of this occupying force reached Fort Malden, the commander there first dispatched an artillery officer to investigate the ice conditions for carrying guns and men to regain the offshore island, then on March 2 sent an expedition of regulars and militia twenty-five miles along the lake to attack at daybreak. In particular, detachments were flung out across the ice to check another retreat by the patriots back to safe American territory. These advanced troops were much outnumbered when the invaders did turn to escape. Yet in a brief but savage fight they filled their purpose, suffering five killed and over twenty wounded; while the fleeing raiders lost eleven dead and far more as wounded or prisoners-- totalling perhaps eighty casualties, though the records are uncertain.[8] At all events, this incisive action, taking in all some thirty hours from Malden to Malden strengthened popular confidence throughout Upper Canada, while the patriots' serious losses and their other failed attempts east and west dampened border adventuring considerably.

In fact, a lull followed; and probably the greatest time of danger in the Rebellion's aftermath had now passed for Upper Canada. In the United States, improved neutrality legislation enacted by Congress that spring not only put new teeth into the endeavours of federal commanders to restrain border raids, but indicated as well that the big American republic was not inclining to declare war. So did the increase in funds and troops also provided to the United States military authorities on the border. Britain, moreover, sent out substantial reinforcements to sustain order along the Canadian side. And in Upper Canada itself a new firm

Lieutenant-Governor, Sir George Arthur, replaced the hopelessly erratic Head, taking office on March 23, 1838. Arthur has often not had a very good standing in Ontario historic lore, largely because of his refusal to intervene in the execution of Samuel Lount and Peter Matthews, the two Yonge Street rebels who were hanged in Toronto that April 12, despite heart-searching pleas on their behalf. Yet the new governor, a conscientious, experienced public servant, was under the strongest instructions to stabilize and uphold constituted authority. He would not begin by overturning a sentence validly reached in the provinces' highest court and after the due process of law. Besides, had Arthur done so, he would most likely have dismayed many more than those who now pled for Lount and Matthews: notably in the exposed areas outside Toronto and along the border, where the limited damage first unleashed by rebellion had swelled into the vandalism, looting and bloodshed of patriot incursions. Justly or not, Upper Canadians far beyond the Family Compact Tories by then would surely and hotly have resented a failure to carry out the court's decision on the two rebel figures -- unfortunate symbols, indeed, of the rash of violence witnessed in Upper Canada since they and their comrades had marched down Yonge Street only a few months earlier.

Furthermore, Arthur himself was no bloody-minded reactionary but a good deal more moderate than many of his provincial Tory officials. His stand on lawful authority made plain, he urged and followed a programme of much greater leniency, wherein transportation generally replaced sentences to death for the major offenders taken in arms while the bulk of Upper Canadians still held in jail were released, and even the lesser American raiders captured were also freed, and returned to the United States. Thee is no time to go into the application of this policy, the leaders' trials - and on occasion their escapes. Suffice it to say that Arthur's competent direction (which actually produced governmental reforms despite the Compact Tories) definitely eased the aftermath, and brightened prospects in Upper Canada.

Very important among these brighter prospects was the coming of Lord Durham as Governor-General for all British North America, and as High Commissioner to investigate the rebellions and their impacts in both Canadas. He landed at Quebec in May, 1838. The appointment of this well-known British radical Liberal to put the colonies to rights certainly unnerved some Upper Canadian Tories, yet Reformers felt a new sweep of hope. Numbers of them more left-wing in outlook had virtually given up on the province, and decided to move to new lands in the American prairies: like James Lesslie, one of three delegates of the Mississippi Emigration Society set up in Toronto who went to choose a farm tract in Iowa. But expectations roused by Durham's name enlivened many of the dejected. One of them, in fact, Francis Hincks, an exponent of the Emigration Society, instead that July set up a

powerful new paper in Toronto, <u>The Examiner</u>, to champion Lord Durham's work, and the 'British Constitutional principle of responsible government'.[9] Durham's visit to Upper Canada in July further heightened Reform expectations -- which finally climaxed when his celebrated report advocating responsible government was received in Upper Canada the following April, 1839.

It is not necessary here to pursue the story and content of Durham's report, which politically put the answer to Rebellion's aftermath. We should rather pursue the continuing story of the patriot raids, which still had two more outbursts to go through before 1838 was out, one in the summer and one in the fall. The lull during the spring, in short, did not become permanent. Nevertheless, to a very large degree the worst was truly over in the border warfare after March, even if one or two of the later assaults were still costly in themselves. The chief reasons have already been suggested; the strengthening of the forces of legitimate order on both sides of the boundary, a positive regime in Upper Canada with real hopes of revived reform and the total discrediting of an older provincial form of radicalism which had turned to freeing Upper Canadians through foreign conquest. Accordingly, we can conclude the warring phases of the aftermath in fairly summary style.

Late in May 1838, violence arose again when the steamer <u>Sir Robert Peel</u> was attacked when it stopped to 'wood-up' on the St. Lawrence islands near Brockville: boarded by Pirate Bill Johnston and his river sea-dogs, who thrust the passengers ashore, then looted and fired the ship to shouts of '<u>Revenge for the Caroline</u>!'.[10] Early in June the so-called Short Hills rising followed in the Niagara back country, after a group of 28 invaders crossed from Grand Island at night under the Irish-American 'colonel' James Morreau. This body was largely composed of former Niagara district inhabitants; and they unquestionably found Canadian sympathizers to hide them in the then-remote inland Short Hills initially settled by American post-Loyalists. However, on June 20 an attack by restive patriots tired of hiding was made on a few Queen's Lancers at an inn that brought search parties rushing down. They soon found and arrested some thirty-four Americans and Canadians, including the Colonel. So much for the 'uprising' now finished. No more consequential was another raid in June, this time across the St. Clair River, which plundered a store at Sombra, killed one local farmer then skeddadled back to Michigan; though not before local inhabitants captured some of the perpetrators. Raiders, in fact, were mainly now to be seen as looters and ruffians, more than any significant threat. And so the border war appeared to have lapsed again-- until the rise of the ominous Hunters Lodges by early autumn.

Here was the purest, least alloyed expression of American expansionism, a semi-secret and semi-military organization that sprung up across the northern states, dedicated to the conquest of Canada. Complete with mystic signs and oaths, the Hunter movement was also a not-untypical American mixture of the gun club, the fraternal order and the activist incendiary society. It even held a grand convention of Lodges in September at Cleveland where it drew up a 'Republican government of Upper Canada', named commanders for the invasion, and erected a bank capitalized at a seven-and-a-half million dollars to fund that operation. The Upper Canadian authorities understandably grew tautly anxious, as rumours of the coming assaults freely circulated about the province. Still, the widely projected Hunters' offensive ended in decisive defeat to east and west: near Prescott in November, at Windsor in December.

As for Prescott, on November 11, 400 Hunters took a ship to cross the St. Lawrence and capture Fort Wellington; but poor co-ordination, the loss of surprise (and some degree of courage) led to only some 170 landing by schooner below the town, where they occupied a heavily built stone windmill. These invaders under the former Polish officer, Nils von Schoultz, held out for four days against militia troops, hoping for reinforcements that never came. Instead, on November 16, regulars arrived with heavy artillery from Kingston. The windmill fortress was battered to surrender; but only after the Upper Canadian forces had suffered sixteen killed and sixty wounded -- quite comparable to British losses at Queenston Heights of fourteen dead and seventy-seven wounded. At his trial, the Hunters' commander, von Schoultz, admitted guilt, declaring he had been misled into believing that a Canada groaning under oppression was only waiting to rise for liberty. But this last idealist in a brigand band was executed in any case; despite the best efforts of the young Kingston lawyer assigned to his defence, John A. Macdonald.[11] Ten other captured Hunter leaders were also hanged, sixty of their followers sentence to transportation to Australia. The Upper Canadian government, facing what was plain brigandage based on no political doctrine except 'we own the continent', had now determined to proceed by court martial and full penalties in order to discourage further bloody onslaughts of this kind.[12]

The next attack at Windsor, completed the work of discouragement. On December 4, Akron lawyer, Lucius V. Bierce commanded a large contingent of Hunters from Michigan, which landed above Windsor, advanced to that village and burned a barracks and a steamer there. Colonel John Prince, by now a militia veteran in the defence of western Upper Canada, summoned up his troops, and near Sandwich inflicted a sharp defeat on the invading force. Its members, those not caught, made for the river, Bierce escaping by canoe. But Bierce's second-in-command a Canadian 'general' William Putnam, lay

dead on the field, as did twenty-five other raiders -- to only four of the militia. Prince also rounded up some forty-six prisoners, six of whom would later hang. He further had five of the prisoners shot out of hand; and whether anything in any way might condone this ruthless decision on the spot, he was to go down in tradition as 'Shot Accordingly Prince'.[13]

Prince's response was assuredly one sign of how far anger, enmity and vengeance might go in an Upper Canada subjected for a year to repeated external threats and destructive attacks. There was little room left for sympathy. Still, the Battle of Windsor proved the last real episode of border war. From the start of 1839 onward any patriot or Hunter activity shrank much farther in futility: scattered into isolated, furtive acts of ruffianism or criminality that had virtually nothing of the redeeming zeal and social purpose of the original Rebellion of 1837 and as its violent aftermath subsided thus, so the aspects of second growth increasingly took over in the province.

By this time, as 1839 went forward, the drastic economic depression of 1837 which had done a great deal to bring on a rebellion in the first place was showing signs of clearing. Immigration from Britain, nearly halted by the bad times and the political disorders in Canada, began to reassert its flow. Trade was recovering, and town and country alike felt the pace of life starting to quicken once more. It still had far to go. Yet from April, 1839, at any rate, knowledge of Durham's recommendation in his report promised not only responsible government and an end to Compact rule, but also a bold new union of the Canadas, which would create a far wider economic unit and enable, with imperial backing, the completion of the vital chain of St. Lawrence canals.

Consequently, by the summer of 1839, Upper Canadian eyes were not looking to vanished border warfare of failed old radicalism, but towards a new era of reform, moderated centrist government and commercial advance. But let the record here turn to Nelson Gorham, still exiled in the United States and writing to his fellow exile and former leader, William Lyon Mackenzie. Reported Gorham on June 2:

> My father was over this spring and I assure you he
> has become quite a comfortable loyalist, so much
> for the magic effect property has upon some minds;
> he is in raptures with Durham's report, and
> sanguinely expects his Lordship will metamorphasize
> the Canadas into a country of liberty, prosperty and
> happiness.[14]

Quite evidently his father's rosy visions had not yet convinced this younger Gorham. Upper Canada, at least, thereafter enjoyed more real liberty, prosperity, and surely

happiness, than it had ever experienced during the rising strains of rebellion -- or amid the far more straining aftermath of border war.

Notes

1. Cited in J.M. Gray, "'General' William Putnam", <u>Ontario History</u>, XLVI 1, Winter 1954, p. 8.

2. J.M.S. Careless, "James Leslie", <u>Dictionary of Canadian Biography</u>, XI (Toronto, 1982), p. 517.

3. As a general account and overview of the aftermath to the Upper Canada Rebellion, this paper is based on major secondary sources rather than primary research; and so it has not been felt necessary to provide extensive footnotes for detailed facts which are well established in these sources. But two things still are necessary here: to note main works that cover the aftermath period in the province and are included in the Suggested Bibliography, and to mark one scholarly work in particular which sets out a very valuable body of primary research, as it proceeds to make a careful, original re-examination of border warfare during that time. To name this particular study first, since I have relied most strongly on it, this is an M.A. thesis completed at the University of Toronto in 1962, by John Parks Martyn, "Upper Canada and Border Incidents, 1837-38: a Study of the Troubles on the American Frontier following the Rebellion of 1837". I have known this study from its start, for it was carried out under my supervision, and have always held it in high regard -- also having hoped it might see publication in toto. Today, however, it has long been left in the academic domain (so to speak), and I am only too glad to make ready use of it now, and to acknowledge fully my debt to what it is, in my opinion, an admirable piece of scholarship. As for the other works utilized, I have included the most significant in the Suggested Bibliography.

4. Craig, <u>Upper Canada</u>, p. 267.

5. See 'The American Steam Packet Coroline Descending the Great Falls of Niagara ... from a sketch by W.R. Collington, Engineer, Boston', reprinted in Margaret Bellasis, <u>Rise, Canadians</u>, (Montreal, 1955), p. 208.

6. Mackenzie to Dr. E. Johnson, January 13, 1838, <u>Mackenzie-Lindsey Papers</u>, Ontario Archives.

7. Martyn, 'Border Incidents', p. 192.

8. <u>Ibid.</u>, pp. 195, 208-9.

9.   This principle was carried at the masterhead of the Examiner from its first issue. See New, <u>Lord Durham</u>, pp. 532, 537, 540.

10. Martyn, p. 268.

11. D.G. Creighton, <u>John A. Macdonald: the Young Politician</u>, (Toronto, 1952), pp. 62-7.

12. Martyn, p. 274.

13. See Alan Douglas, 'The Battle of Windsor', <u>Ontario History</u>, vol. LXI, September 1969, pp. 143-152.

14. Mackenzie-Lindsey Papers.

In Search of Rebellious Relations

J. Brian Gilchrist

The previous papers in this collection have dealt with the people and issues that led to the 1837 conflicts in Upper Canada. This paper suggests some basic resources that will enable readers to trace their genealogy during this period, and perhaps ascertain their family's association, if any, with the "real rebels". Due to space limitations this paper will not deal with land records.[1]

It can be argued that, to a certain degree, many of our immigrant ancestors were rebels. In the old country they could have been rebelling against the authority of established churches that were believed to prohibit personal and spiritual growth. They could have been rebelling against strong aristocratic controls on their lands which had an economic stranglehold on the development of their personal properties and chattels. In other words they were rebelling against the status-quo.

When beginning the quest for ancestors good research guides are invaluable. Genealogy in Ontario: Searching for Records (revised) by Brenda Dougall Merriman[2] is currently the best publication available for Ontario. This guide leads you to a myriad of resources which are available. You should read a general history of the province such as Gerald Craig's Upper Canada: The Formative Years.[3] Any local histories that have been published should be consulted.[4]

Once these preliminary investigations of published sources have started, the clues contained therein allow you to begin your original research. In genealogy your searches should progress from the known to the unknown. Thus try and start with the last possible fact that could have happened to an ancestor -- death. If your ancestor was fortunate enough to have been memorialized on a tombstone the inscription could be as simple as: "In Memory of John Long who died Jan. 22, 1874 aged 69 years", or the following partial inscription on one stone:

"Samuel Lount was the eldest son of the late GABRIEL LOUNT, an Englishman, who emigrated to Pennsylvania

in the middle of the 18th century, and of
PHILADELPHIA HUGHES his wife a Quakeress. He
emigrated to Upper Canada and settled near Newmarket
in the County of York, in 1811. In 1834, he was
elected to represent the County of Simcoe, in the
Upper Canada Legislature, and served two years. In
1836, he became a candidate again, but was defeated
by corrupt practices used by his political
opponents. A petition of 8,000 people asked for a
reprieve, which was refused. He lived a patriot,
and died for popular rights.[5]

The varying amount of detail on these two tombstones is
obvious. Upon further investigation the term "died for
popular rights" will be found to mean that he was hanged for
the crime of high treason!

The Ontario Genealogical Society (O.G.S.) and its 27
branches across the province have been transcribing the
tombstones in Ontario's cemeteries for several years. Copies
may be found at the National Archives of Canada, Ottawa;
Archives of Ontario, Toronto; and the Canadiana Collection of
the North York Public Library. The latter also houses the
Ontario Genealogical Society's library.

Once the date of death has been obtained from a tombstone
or other source, the researcher could attempt to locate a will
if one exists at the Archives of Ontario. Some wills can also
be found at the local Land Registry Office if the deceased
owned property. Catherine Shepard's Surrogate Court Records
at the Archives of Ontario, as published by the O.G.S., will
guide the researcher seeking these types of documents.

Retrospective files of newspapers are another source of
information of use to a genealogist. There are several
problems associated with newspaper research, the following
being but a few examples: bias -- usually political. If your
ancestor was an Irish Roman Catholic Reformer and the editor
of the local newspaper was Scottish Presbyterian Tory do not
be disappointed if you do not find a large glowing obituary.
Be satisfied with "Died recently, at an advanced age, the
result of an accident, Mr. Kennedy", or else be prepared for
nothing at all! The reverse could be true; the editor could
be so pleased that the "old so and so" was dead, it could be
front page news!

Credibility is another problem with newspaper research.
Occasionally statements of deaths, marriages or other
newsworthy items that were reported to have happened were in
later issues retracted. e.g. "Your recent mentioned notice of
my untimely death is not true".

Reliability of relationships can be questioned. For
example, not mentioning all of the living children of the

deceased in an obituary. Some of these types of errors were by commission rather than omission. Spelling of names and places can be very phonic, and thus subject to error. For example, "Longale" may mean Longueuil, whereas "of Hamilton", may refer either to Hamilton Township or the town of Hamilton.

Newspapers are the day-to-day diaries of their communities that chronicle events of local, national and international importance. For the purposes of local history, as well as genealogy these back issues are invaluable. The following news item from the Cobourg Star of December 27th, 1837 (as previously reported in the Belleville Intellegencer), relates the story of a death which can be directly attributed to the rebellious events which occurred on Yonge Street during that infamous first week of December 1837:

> On the night of Friday, 15th inst., Capt. James MacNab, in command of a picket guard at Young's tavern, was accidentally wounded, when a young man ran against him with a bayonet, and died on the following day, the 16th. He and his father represented the County of Hastings in the Provincial Parliament.

The major obstacle for the use of newspapers is the location of extant files. In 1987 a publication appeared which has helped to alleviate this situation. The Inventory of Ontario Newspapers, 1793 - 1986, First Edition, 1987[6] by J. Brian Gilchrist surveyed 325 libraries and archives across Canada, as well as the British Newspaper Library, for details of their original and microform holdings. A companion publication to the above inventory, is the Checklist of Canadian Newspaper Indexes prepared by Sandra Burrows and Franceen Gaudet of the National Library of Canada[7] which details the location and scope of various newspaper indexes which are available across the country.

Thomas B. Wilson, of Hunterdon House, Lambertville , New Jersey, has published several volumes of early Ontario newspaper death notices which are of use to the genealogist. (see Suggested Bibliography)

Religious records are a useful resource for the family historian. The most often consulted are the baptism/christening, and marriage registers. A variety of other registers were maintained such as communion rolls, confirmation lists, Sunday School registers etc. Most of these records are ignored, much to the loss of the researcher. For example, I am seeking the early registers of Norval and Union Presbyterian Church in Esquesing Township, Halton County. The baptismal registers begin in the early 1850s-- but the congregation is several years older. In reading the Session minutes I found a statement that a letter had been written to the Reverend Peter Gray "formerly of this congregation but now of the Beckwith charge" (some 300 miles to the east of Norval) asking for the return of the baptismal, marriage and other registers he took with him upon his leaving. Therefore earlier records did exist but their current location is unknown.

By making contact with the respective denominational archives it might be possible to ascertain the location of known registers, and congregations. Contact should also be made with the local branches of the Ontario Genealogical Society as many members are involved in church register transcription projects.

The previous pages have attempted to act as a guide for the beginning genealogist searching ancestry anywhere in the province of Upper Canada. For those searching in the Home District (the area including and immediately surrounding Metro Toronto) the following publications should be consulted: Ontario Genealogical Society's, Toronto Branch, reprint of the <u>1837 Directory of York and the Home District</u>[8] (although actually prepared in late 1836), as well as the <u>Potters Field</u>[9] burial register, and <u>Rebels Arrested in Upper Canada 1837-1838</u>.[10]

It would be remiss to conclude this paper without mentioning the two-volume publication titled <u>Guide to the Holdings of the Archives of Ontario</u>. Copies are available on microfiche for purchase by individuals or local libraries. This institution houses not only the bulk of Ontario land records, wills and newspapers but also a collection of pre-civil registration marriage records as well as the majority of extant census records.

In conclusion, genealogists researching Ontario ancestry are indeed fortunate to have a multitude of records available to research in. Unlike so many other regions of the world, that have lost a wealth of research material during various wars and insurrections, the existence of democratic principles in Canada has helped ensure freedom of access to the existing records. These principles for which our ancestors fought are in danger of being trampled underfoot as federal and provincial governments introduce so-called "freedom of access to information" legislation to actually reduce the number of documents about people in Ontario's past available to those seeking their ancestors, rebellious or otherwise.

Notes

1. Lillian F. Gates, <u>Land Policies of Upper Canada</u>, (Toronto: University of Toronto Press, 1968).

2. Brenda Dougall Merriman, <u>Genealogy in Ontario: Searching the Records</u> (revised), (Toronto: Ontario Genealogy Society, 1988).

3. Gerald Craig, <u>Upper Canada: The Formative Years, 1784-1841</u>, (Toronto: McClelland and Stewart, 1963).

4. William E. Morley, <u>Canadian Local Histories to 1950: A Bibliography</u>, (Toronto: University of Toronto Press, 1978), vol. 3, <u>Ontario and the Canadian North</u>.

5. Necropolis Cemetery, Toronto. (Lount and Mathews were originally buried in the Potter's Field at Yonge and Bloor streets on 13th April 1838).

6. J. Brian Gilchrist, ed. & comp. <u>Inventory of Ontario Newspapers 1793-1986</u>, (Toronto: Micromedia, 1988).

7. Sandra Burrows and Franceen Gaudet, <u>Checklist of Canadian Newspapers</u>, (Ottawa: National Library of Canada, 1987).

8. George Walton, <u>City of Toronto and the Home District Commercial Directory and Register...for 1837</u>, (repr.), (Toronto: Toronto Branch, Ontario Genealogical Society, 1987).

9. Elizabeth Hancocks C.G. ed. and comp., <u>Potter's Field Cemetery 1826-1855</u>, (Toronto: Generation Press, 1983).

10. <u>Rebels Arrested in Upper Canada</u>, (Toronto: Ontario Genealogical Society, Toronto Branch, 1987).

Contributors

Dr. Anthony Adamson is a restoration architect, author and lecturer.

Melody Brown is the Administrative Assistant for the Ontario Black History Society

E. Jayne Cardno is the curatorial advisor to the Van Egmond Foundation in Seaforth, and attends the University of Western Ontario.

Dr. J.M.S. Careless is Professor Emeritus, University of Toronto.

John Carter is a Museums Development Officer for the Ontario Ministry of Culture and Communications, and former Curator of the John R. Park Homestead museum in Essex County.

Dorothy Duncan is the Executive Director of The Ontario Historical Society.

Mary Beacock Fryer is the author of several books about pre-Confederation Ontario history including <u>Volunteers and Redcoats, Rebels and Raiders: A Military History of the Upper Canadian Rebellion</u>.

Douglas Fyfe was the senior historical interpreter at The Gibson House museum in Willowdale at the time of the 1837 Rebellion Conference, and is now a member of the staff at Historic Fort York, Toronto.

J. Brian Gilchrist is a professional genealogist and compiler of a recent inventory of Ontario newspapers.

Cecil Houston is a Professor of Geography at Erindale College, University of Toronto.

Joyce Lewis is a researcher, lecturer and author about 19th Century domestic life, and former Convenor of Friends of the Hutchison House museum, Peterborough.

Dr. Glenn Lockwood is the author of several books about Eastern Ontario, a lecturer at the History Department, University of Ottawa, and former Publications Chairman of The Ontario Historical Society.

Allan McGillivray is the Curator of the Uxbridge-Scott Historical Society Museum.

Joan Murray is Curator of Toronto's First Post Office.

Bruce Peel is a former librarian who was in charge of the Adam Shortt Collection of Canadiana at the University of Saskatchewan, and later a staff member and Chief Librarian at the University of Alberta.

Elinor Kyte Senior is a Professor of History at St. Francis Xavier University, Antigonish, Nova Scotia and author of Redcoats and Patriotes: The Rebellion in Lower Canada 1837-38.

Professor Ronald Stagg teaches history at Ryerson Polytechnical Institute in Toronto an is co-author of The Rebellion of 1837 in Upper Canada.

Duncan Urquhart was Education Co-ordinator at the Enoch Turner Schoolhouse, Toronto at the time of the 1837 Rebellion Remembered Conference, and is now working for Alberta Culture researching educational programmes for a proposed agricultural museum at Wetaskiwin, Alberta.

Sarah Walker is Executive Assistant of the Ontario Museums Association.

****

The Ontario Historical Society recommends the special issue of The York Pioneer, 1987, Volume 82, that contains several articles about the 1837 Rebellion in Upper Canada, and its aftermath. Enquiries about this publication should be directed to The York Pioneer and Historical Society, Box 481, Station K, Toronto, Ontario, M4P 2G9.

Suggested Bibliography

Abrahamson, U., <u>God Bless Our Homes</u>. Toronto, 1966.

Aitken, Barbara B., <u>Local Histories of Ontario Municipalities, 1851-1977: A Bibliography</u>. Toronto, 1978.

Althouse, J.G., <u>The Ontario Teacher: An Historical Account of Progress</u>. Doctoral Thesis, University of Toronto, 1929. Reprinted London, England: W.J. Gage Ltd., 1967.

Arnold, Janet., <u>Patterns of Fashions I, 1660-1860</u>. London, 1972.

Boggs, Winthrop S., <u>The Postal Stamp and Postal History of Canada</u>. Lawrence, Mass. 1975.

Burnham, Dorothy K., <u>Cut my Cote</u>. Toronto: Royal Ontario Museum, 1973.

Burnham, Harold B. and Dorothy K., <u>'Keep Me Warm One Night': Early Handweaving in Eastern Canada</u>. Toronto: University of Toronto, 1972.

Burrows, Sandra and Gaudet, Franceen, <u>Checklist of Canadian Newspapers</u>. Ottawa, 1987.

Careless, J.M.S., "James Lesslie", <u>Dictionary of Canadian Biography</u>. XI, Toronto, 1982.

Clark, S.D., <u>Movements of Political Protest in Canada, 1640-1840</u>. Toronto, 1959.

Corey, Albert B., <u>The Crisis of 1830-42 in Canadian-American Relations</u>. New Haven, 1944.

Craig, Gerald, <u>Upper Canada: the Formative Years, 1784-1841</u>. Toronto, 1903.

Creighton, D.G., <u>John A. Macdonald: the Young Politician</u>. Toronto, 1952.

Dent, J.C., <u>The Story of the Upper Canada Rebellion</u>. Toronto, 1885.

Douglas, R. Alan, ed., <u>John Prince</u>. Toronto, 1980.

Douglas, R. Alan, "The Battle of Windsor", <u>Ontario History</u>.
     LXI, September 1969.

Dunham, Aileen, <u>Political Unrest in Upper Canada 1815-1836.</u>
     McClelland and Stewart, 1963.

Fairley, Margaret, <u>The Selected Writings of William Lyon
     Mackenzie</u>. Oxford University Press, Toronto, 1960.

Finley, Gerald, <u>George Heriot: Postmaster-Painter of the
     Canadas</u>. University of Toronto Press, Toronto, 1983.

Firth, E.G., <u>The Town of York 1815-1834</u>. The Champlain
     Society, University of Toronto Press, 1966.

<u>First Report on the Committee on Finance, Post Office
     Department</u>. Submitted March, 1836, privately printed and
     distributed by Allan L. Steinhart, Toronto, 1985.

Foster, Vanda. <u>A Visual History of Costume: The Nineteenth
     Century</u>. London, 1984.

Gates, Lillian F., <u>Land Policies of Upper Canada</u>.   Toronto,
     1968.

Gidney, R.D. "Elementary Education in Upper Canada: A
     Reassessment." <u>Ontario History</u>. LXV, 3, September 1973.

Gilchrist, J. Brian, ed. & comp. <u>Inventory of Ontario
     Newspapers</u>. Toronto, 1988.

Glazebrook, G.T. deT. <u>The Story of Toronto</u>. University of
     Toronto Press, 1971.

Godfrey, Sheldon & Judy, <u>Stones, Bricks and History</u>.   Lester
     and Orpen Dennys, Toronto, 1984.

Gray, J.M.   "'General' William Putnam." <u>Ontario History</u>.
     XLVI, 1, Winter 1954.

Guillet, E.C., <u>The Lines and Times of the Patriots</u>.   Toronto,
     1968.

Guillet, Edwin C., <u>Pioneer Travel in Upper Canada</u>.
     University of Toronto Press, Toronto, 1933.

Hancocks, Elizabeth C.G. ed. and comp., <u>Potter's Field
     Cemetery 1826-1855</u>. Toronto, 1983.

Harrison, Horace W., "Money Letters", <u>PHSC Journal</u>.   June
     1987.

Hodgins, J. George, ed. <u>A Documentary History of Education in Upper Canada from the Passing of the Constitutional Act of 1791 to the Close of the Reverend Doctor Ryerson's Administration of the Education Department in 1876.</u> Toronto, Warwick Bros. and Rutter, 1894, Volumes I-X.

Jameson, A., <u>Winter Studies and Summer Rambles in Canada</u>. London, 1838.

Kerr, W.B., "The Canada Company and Anthony Van Egmond", <u>The Huron Expositor</u>. Seaforth, 1931. Weldon Library, University of Western Ontario.

Kinchen, Oscar A., <u>The Rise and Fall of the Patriot Hunters</u>. New York, 1956.

Landon, Fred, <u>An Exile From Canada</u>. Toronto, 1960.

Lindsey, Charles, <u>The Life and Times of William Lyon Mackenzie</u>. Toronto, 1862.

Lizars, Rovina and Kathleen, <u>Humours of '37</u>. Toronto, 1897.

Marsh, Robert, <u>Seven Years of My Life or a Narrative of a Partiot Exile</u>. Buffalo, 1848.

Martyn, J.P., "The Patriot Invasion of Pelee Island", <u>Ontario History</u>. September, 1964.

McFall, David and Jean, <u>Land Records in Ontario Registry Offices</u>. Ontario Genealogical Society Toronto Branch, 1984.

McGuire, L. Ronald, "Private Messenger and Public Servants: Carrying the Mails in Pre-Confederation Ontario", <u>By River, Road and Rail: Transportation in 19th Century Ontario</u>. Ontario Museum Association, 1984.

McKenzie, Donald A., <u>Death Notices from the Christian Guardian</u>. 1836-50, 1982; 1851-60, 1984.

Mckenzie, Donald A., <u>More Notices from Methodist Newspapers</u>. 1830-57, 1986.

McLoed, Donald, <u>A Brief Review of the Settlement in Upper Canada</u>. Belleville, 1972.

Merriman, Brenda Dougall, <u>Genealogy in Ontario: Searching the Records</u>. (revised), Toronto, 1988.

Miller, Audrey Saunders, ed. <u>The Journals of Mary O'Brien</u>. MacMillan of Canada, 1968.

Miller, Linus W., <u>Notes of an Exile to Van Dieman's Land</u>. Fredonia, New York, 1846.

Moodie, S., <u>Life in the Clearings</u>. London, 1853.

        <u>Roughing it in The Bush</u>. Toronto, 1913 (1st ed. 1852).

Morley, William E., <u>Canadian Local Histories to 1950: A Bibliography</u>. vol. 3, Toronto, 1978.

News, Chester A., <u>Lord Durham</u>. Oxford, 1929.

<u>Notices and Forms used in the Duke Street Post Office 1833-39</u>. Reprinted by the Town of York Historical Society, 1983.

Parvin, Viola Elizabeth, <u>Authorization of Textbooks for the Schools of Ontario</u>. Toronto, University of Toronto Press, 1965.

Pope, John, "The Enoch Turner Schoolhouse: 1848." <u>The York Pioneer</u>. 1971.

Prentice, Alison L. and Susan E. Houston, eds., <u>Family, School and Society in Nineteenth Century Canada.</u> Toronto, Oxford University Press, 1975.

Preston, T.R., <u>Three Years' Residence in Canada From 1837-1839</u>. London, 1840.

Read, C. and Stagg, R.J., <u>The Rebellion of 1837 in Upper Canada</u>. Toronto and Ottawa, 1985.

Read, C., <u>The Rising in Western Upper Canada 1837-8: The Duncombe Revolt and After</u>. Toronto, 1982.

<u>Rebels Arrested in Upper Canada</u>. Ontario Genealogical Society Toronto Branch, 1987.

<u>Report of the Select Committee of Upper Canada, April 30, 1839</u>. Cited in Tiffany, Orrin Edward, <u>The Canadian Rebellion of 1837-38</u>. Buffalo, 1905.

Robertson, John Ross, <u>Landmarks of Toronto</u>. Vols. I and III Mika Publishing Company, Belleville, 1974, 1976-facsimile.

Robertson, Virginia R. ed., <u>Upper Canada in the 1830s Documents in Canada Series</u>. Toronto, Ontario Institute for Studies in Education, 1977.

Ross, Robert B., <u>The Patriot Wars</u>. Lansing, 1894.

Shannon, William, <u>The Dominion Orange Harmonist</u>. Toronto, 1876.

Shea, B., <u>History of the Sheas and Birth of a Township</u>. Peterborough, 1965.

Smith, William, <u>History of the Post Office in British North America 1839-70</u>. Cambridge University Press, 1920.

Snow, Samuel, <u>The Exile's Return, or Narrative of Samuel Snow</u>. Cleveland, 1846.

Stagg, R.J. "1837 Revisited", in <u>The York Pioneer</u>. 1987.

Stewart, Frances, <u>Our Forest Home</u>. ed. S. Dunlop, Montreal, 1902.

Suggitt, G., <u>Roses and Thorns</u>. Peterborough, 1972.

<u>The Dismissal of James S. Howard Esq.</u> Toronto, 1839 Reprinted by the Town of York Historical Society, 1983.

Theller, Edward A., <u>Canada in 1837-38: Showing by Historical Facts, the Causes of the Late Attempted Revolution and Its Failure</u>. Philadelphia, 1841.

Tiffany, Orrin Edward, <u>The Canadian Rebellion of 1837-38</u>. Buffalo, 1905.

Traill, C.P., <u>The Canadian Settler's Guide</u>. Toronto, 1969, (1st ed. 1855).

      <u>The Backwoods of Canada</u>. Toronto: McClelland and Stewart, 1966.

Van Egmond Papers, Public Archives of Canada.

Walton, George, <u>City of Toronto and the Home District Commercial Directory and Register...for 1837</u>. Ontario Genealogical Society, Toronto Branch, 1987.

Wilson, J. Donald, "The Teacher in Early Ontario" in <u>Aspects of Nineteenth Century Ontario</u>. eds. F.H. Armstrong et al. Toronto, University of Toronto Press, 1974.

Wilson, Thomas B., <u>Marriage Bonds of Ontario</u>. 1803-34, 1985.

      <u>Ontario Marriage Notices</u>. 1982.

      and Wilson, Emily, <u>Directory of the Province of Ontario 1857</u>. 1987.